EDWARD III

EDWARD III
Monarch of Chivalry

Bryan Bevan

The Rubicon Press

For Sadika Tancred

The Rubicon Press
57 Cornwall Gardens
London SW7 4BE

© Bryan Bevan, 1992

A catalogue record for this book is available from the British Library.

Printed and bound in Great Britain by Biddles Limited of Guildford and King's Lynn

Contents

List of Illustrations

Tomb of Edward II in Gloucester Cathedral. *By courtesy of the National Monuments Record.*

Execution of Hugh Despenser the Younger in 1326. *By courtesy of the Bibliothèque Nationale, Paris.*

Corbel head of Edward III from Tewkesbury Abbey. *By courtesy of the National Monuments Record.*

Battle of Poitiers. *By courtesy of the British Library Board.*

A meeting of the Knights of the Garter in the chapel of St. George at Windsor. *By courtesy of the British Library Board.*

Effigy of the Black Prince. *By courtesy of the National Portrait Gallery.*

The Black Prince pays homage to Edward III. *By courtesy of the British Library Board.*

Gilt bronze tomb effigy of King Edward III. *By courtesy of the Dean and Chapter of Westminster.*

Cover illustration: Portrait of Edward III. *By courtesy of the Dean and Chapter of Windsor.*

Acknowledgements

To the Very Reverend Patrick Mitchell, Dean of Windsor for showing me the picture of Edward III in the Deanery drawing-room, Windsor Castle.

To the archivist, Dr. Eileen Scarff, the Chapter Office, the Cloisters, Windsor Castle for much help and advice.

To Ann Holland for kindly lending her invaluable copies of the Works of Jean Froissart.

To the Keeper of the Muniments, Westminster Abbey, and to Mrs. Nixon, assistant librarian for her help.

To the London Library for their constant help.

To my sister Winfreda Murray for helping with the page proofs.

To my friend Andrew Low for accompanying me to the sites of the Battles of Crécy and Poitiers and to Windsor on one occasion.

Lastly to my publishers and friends of The Rubicon Press, Juanita Homan and Anthea Page for their courtesy, help and loyalty.

I Dishonourable Inheritance

Prince Edward, eldest son of Edward II, and of Isabella of France, daughter of Philip IV, destined to be one of England's most spectacular kings, was born at 5.30 a.m. on November 13th 1312 at Windsor. That year was a tragic one for Edward of Caernarvon (he was born there), for six months earlier his great favourite Piers Gaveston had been treacherously murdered on Blacklow Hill near Warwick through the machinations of his rebellious cousin Thomas of Lancaster and powerful barons. Though Edward swore to avenge Gaveston's death, the birth of a son and heir to some extent mitigated his grief. He was certainly judicious in rejecting the suggestions of his Francophile courtiers that the infant prince should be called Louis. Instead, he was named Edward, his own name and that of his grandfather who was perhaps the greatest of the Plantagenets. To signify his pleasure, the King bestowed annual pensions of twenty pounds per annum on John Lounges, Queen Isabella's valet and his wife.

Isabella was aged only twelve when four years earlier she had married Edward II in the Church of Notre Dame in Boulogne on January 25th 1308. However, during Edward's coronation at Westminster she soon became aware, as did her French entourage, that the first place in his affections was held by Gaveston, a Gascon of good family with a waspish tongue, detested by the old nobility. Their love for one another somewhat resembled the biblical story of David and Jonathan, "a love which surpassed the love of women". It was natural for a young bride to dwell on her injured feelings, observing that her husband preferred Gaveston's bed to her own. So she complained furiously to her father Philip the Fair that Edward was not only giving away her father's wedding presents, but even her jewels to his minion. There is a list of the Queen's jewellery

1

in the French Archives Nationales, and the royal chamberlain Hugues de Bouville was the official responsible for the purchases. They included not only jewels, crowns and trinkets, but also vestments and furniture for the royal chapel, household linen and horses for conveying Isabella and her household to England.[1]

Since Edward II's homosexuality and his incompetence to govern were later factors in his Deposition, in raising his eldest son Prince Edward to the throne, it is fitting to discuss what his contemporaries thought of his eccentricities. Edward might have made an admirable country squire, living in his favourite home of Langley in Hertfordshire, but he was absolutely unsuited to be a mediaeval king. Higden wrote: "Undervaluing the society of the magnates, he fraternized with buffoons and singers, actors, carters, ditchers, oarsmen, sailors, and others who practised mechanical arts." A mediaeval king was expected to delight in jousting and tournaments, and to be at least war-like. After England's ignominious defeat by the Scots at Bannockburn (1314), Robert le Messager, a nuncio in Edward's court, was talking one day with the sub-bailiff of Newington near Sittingbourne in Kent, and strongly criticizing the King. "Nobody need expect the King to win battles, if he spends the time when he ought to be hearing mass in idling and applying himself to making ditches and digging and other improper occupations."

Edward III certainly learnt from his father's mistakes never to undervalue the society of his magnates, for they were loyally to support him throughout his reign where they had treacherously rebelled against and deserted his father. On occasions Edward II was capable of better behaviour, for Thomas of Cobham, Bishop of Worcester, told the Pope that during a session of Parliament (October 1320) that "he is behaving magnificently and contrary to his former custom, he is getting up early in the morning."[2]

Edward's homosexuality has probably been exaggerated, for he was also a heterosexual. Besides his eldest son, he had three children by Isabella, John of Eltham born in 1316, and two daughters Eleanor of Woodstock, later married to the Count of

2

Gelderland, and Joan of the Tower, wedded when barely an infant to David Bruce, King of Scotland.

In his dramatic work *The Tragedy of Edward II* Christopher Marlowe, using Stow and Holinshed, reveals a more intuitive understanding of and compassion for Prince Edward's father than the King's contemporaries. He is more alive to the tragedy of his life. In a sense Gaveston seems to dominate the play, whether living or dead. He puts into Gaveston's mouth:

> I must have wanton poets
> > pleasant wits
> Musicians that with touching of a
> > string,
> May draw the pliant King which way
> > I please,
> Music and poetry is his delight.[3]

Edward II's artistic tastes included a love of music for he became a patron of musicians and minstrels, taking an eager interest in the early form of the violin known to the Welsh as 'the crwth'. This endeared our first Prince of Wales to his Welsh subjects, the only ones to mourn his later tragic loss. Prince Edward's feeling for the dramatic as Edward III, his love of splendour, and his delight in music and song when abroad on his campaigns owed something to his father. Marlowe portrays Prince Edward as a more determined character than the historical immature Edward, less dominated by the vengeful, ruthless Queen Isabella, his mother. Early in his life in his apparent submission to the wishes of his mother and her atrocious lover Roger Mortimer, he seems a traitor to his father.

In his choice of his son's tutor, Edward II acted wisely. He appointed the scholarly bibliophile, Richard Hungerville, better known as Richard de Bury, later (1333) Bishop of Durham, the author of *The Philobiblion* and an avid book collector. He had served as English ambassador to France, Hainault and Germany, and held many high offices, but in his rare moments of leisure he liked nothing so much as to buy books along the Left Bank in his beloved Paris. Edward spoke several languages, English, French, and possessed some knowledge of

3

German and Flemish. That he both spoke and wrote Latin was entirely due to his tutor. Edward's accomplishments were those expected of a fourteenth century prince, hawking, coursing, hunting, dancing, singing and, above all, skill in handling the sword, lance and long-bow. Perhaps Prince Edward's most valuable lesson was to learn by his father's follies. No successful ruler in England could prosper without the counsel and consent of his nobles. In his later creation when King, of his younger brother John of Eltham as Earl of Cornwall[4], he was mindful of his father's subjects' open contempt when he gave this title to Gaveston. An early companion selected by his father was Griffin, son of Griffin of Wales.

His mother Queen Isabella, best known in history as "She-wolf of France"[5], was a woman of beauty and charm and some intelligence, but she was passionate, querulous and a cunning dissembler. A dominating character such as Isabella's needs a masterful man to subdue her, and she was later to find such a man in her lover Roger Mortimer, whose influence on his royal mistress was evil and malignant. Her intrigues against her husband are only partly excusable, but her later treasonable conduct cannot possibly be justified. However, for a time after Gaveston's murder, she acted as peace-maker between Edward II and the barons. A bitter civil war eventually broke out between the King's cousin, Thomas Earl of Lancaster, leader of the disaffected nobles and the King, but at the Battle of Boroughbridge (1322) north-west of York, Lancaster was defeated. Falling into Edward's hands, the rebel was beheaded without trial outside his own Castle of Pontefract. It was after Boroughbridge that Edward's relations with his Queen sharply deteriorated.

Isabella had been treated by no means ungenerously, for she had been given on marriage a splendid domestic household of her own of two hundred people and endowed with the revenues of the counties of Ponthieu and Montreuil. However, after 1322, she deeply resented her husband's ministers, Sir Hugh Despenser the elder, later created Earl of Winchester, and his son Sir Hugh Despenser the younger, a contemporary of Edward's. They were certainly loyal to the King, but he was

4

far too generous in rewarding them. Isabella hated them. Though reputed to have been the King's lover, there is no real evidence that there was a homosexual relationship between Edward and the younger Sir Hugh. The King married his new favourite to his great-niece Eleanor, one of the heiresses of Gilbert de Clare, Earl of Gloucester. If their relationship was stronger than friendship, it is significant that the Earl of Pembroke warned Edward in 1321 that "he perishes on the rocks that loves another more than himself". Isabella clearly suspected that Despenser was her husband's lover.

Both Despensers were avaricious for estates and land. Not only did the younger Despenser become Lord of Glamorgan by his marriage, but he persuaded King Edward to grant him the Castle of Drystillwyn in Wales and even the Isle of Lundy. Wishing to insure himself against the possibility of his downfall, Despenser deposited enormous sums of money with the Florentine banking houses of Bardi and Peruzzi. His cupidity earned him the jealousy and dislike of the magnates. None of the Despensers' enemies were more ruthless than the two powerful marcher lords, Roger Mortimer of Chirk and his nephew Roger Mortimer of Wigmore. They had both given Edward notable service in Wales and Ireland, ruling North Wales almost as independent princes. Later, however, they violently opposed the King and the Despensers on being captured, languished in the Tower of London for two years in about 1322.

The young Sir Hugh, an efficient administrator,[6] made the fatal mistake of underestimating the Queen. Sensing the deterioration of the relationship between their master and the Queen, both Despensers advised Edward to sequestrate her estates, arguing that there was serious danger of a French invasion. After all, Isabella was French by birth. Then the younger Sir Hugh's wife was appointed Isabella's housekeeper, to spy on this proud, passionate woman and to censure all her correspondence. Hugh Despenser tried to obtain a papal annulment of Edward's marriage.

When Charles IV, Isabella's surviving brother, succeeded to the throne of France in 1322, he politely reminded his

5

brother-in-law Edward that he owed him fealty for English possessions in France, for the rich wine-producing province of Gascony and for Ponthieu. He suggested that Edward meet him in Amiens during the Easter of 1324. Gascony was for many years an incessant bone of contention between the two countries, especially when serious incidents erupted on its border. When Charles IV invaded Edward's duchy of Gascony during August, matters became even more critical. Unfortunately Aymer de Valence, Earl of Pembroke, a leading statesman entrusted with a mission to France, died suddenly after landing in the country. The Despensers agreed with Pope John XXII's suggestion that Isabella should go on a diplomatic mission to try to mediate between the two countries. It was a fatal error and misjudgement on their part to allow Isabella to go to France.

A born intriguer, she was already the head of a powerful faction consisting of her husband's and the Despensers' enemies and determined to oppose the King and to ruin the Despensers. These conspirators included Adam of Orleton, Bishop of Hereford, a protégé of Roger Mortimer of Wigmore, a learned man, but subtle intriguer. Others were Henry Burghersh, Bishop of Lincoln and John of Droxford, Bishop of Bath and Wells. Henry of Leicester, the younger brother of the executed Thomas of Lancaster, when sounded, promised his support.

Earlier, on the night of August 1st 1324, during the feast of St. Peter and Vincula, Roger Mortimer of Wigmore (on Lammas day according to John Stow's *Chronicles*[7]) succeeded in escaping from the Tower, an extremely difficult feat and cleverly contrived. He owed his freedom mainly to Orleton, the Bishop of Hereford, and Gerald de Alspaye, sub-lieutenant in the Tower, who on the fateful night introduced a powerful drug, "a sleepe-drink" according to Stow into his guards' drink as they were celebrating the feast. As the men lurched across the courtyards of the Tower and in their stupor sank to the ground, Mortimer escaped by rope-ladder over the walls, and then by boat on the Thames to the south bank. On horseback he galloped to Porchester where he took ship for France, managing to ingratiate himself with Charles IV. Enfeebled by the hardships of his confinement, the elder Mortimer of Chirk later died in the Tower. Exactly when Queen Isabella became Mortimer's lover it is impossible to say, whether in France or earlier.

In September 1325 Prince Edward, an intelligent handsome boy, was almost thirteen. He must have been aware of the extremely strained relations between his father and mother. How often had he heard his mother express her contempt for his father. Again at court, Edward's inadequacy as King was often discussed. Now she was in Paris and by midsummer she had succeeded in reaching an agreement with the French. The occupied Territories would be restored to Edward, provided he came to France to render homage for them. According to Murimuth the contemporary chronicler, this was much debated. However, the Despensers, fearful lest their many enemies wreak vengeance on them once their friend, the King was out of their sight, dissuaded him from going. It was the papal nuncios who first suggested that Prince Edward should deputize for his father. This absolutely suited Isabella's secret plans. His father and the Council agreed to it.

There exists a very interesting account of the household expenses of Edward of Windsor from August 12th to September 11th 1325, the day before he sailed to join his mother in France and to render homage in place of his father for Aquitaine and Ponthieu. The Prince's household was highly organized.[8] There were five departments, with a clerk at the head of each wardrobe, marshalsea, kitchen, pantry and buttery. The Clerk of the Kitchen was at the head of six sub-departments, the great kitchen, the larder, the salary, the scutellary, the Poultry Office and *Aula et Camera*. The Treasurer was an important official, William de Cusaunce who controlled the main funds. Edward's party - he was accompanied by one of his father's few loyal bishops closely attached to the Court - Walter Stapledon of Exeter - started from Stratford (now West Ham) on August 12th taking the main pilgrim route through Rochester, Bromley, Sevenoaks, Leeds Castle and Canterbury to Dover. Queen Isabella had her own messenger included in the party, charged with bringing her letters. Details are given of the alms at the Tomb of St. Thomas the Martyr at Canterbury and of the horses borrowed from the Abbot of Christ Church Canterbury (August 24th). Curious items are Prince Edward's new bed costing £38.12.6d and mention of two penocels worked with his arms for the Trumpeters. Three dozen pairs of shoes and of gloves were bought for a few shillings. There were special payments for people not subordinate to any department such as huntsmen, falconers and messengers. A comparison of the expenses of Edward of Windsor's household in 1325 shows that they more or less tally with those of his father Edward of Caernarvon in 1285-89. The expenses are £4,000 per annum. Two carts were needed to carry the personal luggage (harnesium) of the royal party while each department required a cart of its own. Five sumpter horses and a cart-horse were bought on August 30th on the wardrobe account at the cost of £25.6s. and fourteen sumpter horses sufficed for the kitchen account.

Prince Edward now joined his mother in Paris. A boy of almost thirteen is not too young to be unaware of his mother's adulterous relations with the traitor Roger Mortimer, banished the realm of England by his father. On September 21st Edward performed his act of homage to Charles IV his uncle at the Castle of Bois de Vincennes outside Paris.

Froissart relates that Isabella and her son were at first most affectionately received by her brother Charles IV. "The King toke her in his armes, and kyst her, and sayd 'Ye be welcome feyre Sister with my feyre nephew...demanding right swetely of her astate and busyness'." The Queen always ready to air her grievances, tearfully complained of "all the felonyes and injuries done to her by Sir Hewe Spenser, requesting her brother's aid and silence." Isabella, an accomplished actress knew instinctively how to play on the sympathy of others.

A dangerous group of Edward II's enemies joined Queen Isabella in Paris. These included her lover Roger Mortimer, Stratford Bishop of Winchester, Airwyn Bishop of Norwich and even the King's half-brother Edmund of Kent[9], incensed because he had been criticized by Edward for his disastrous campaign in Gascony.

The watchful Bishop Stapledon, who had escorted Prince Edward to France, soon became aware that Lord Mortimer was living in open adultery with Queen Isabella. Stapledon's own life was in danger. On one occasion a brick from a scaffolding fell close to his head, and a footbridge gave way under the bishop's mule as he followed on foot. He soon possessed evidence that treason was being plotted in Paris. The Queen and Mortimer were planning to return to England with armed men to oust Hugh Despenser as the King of England's chief adviser. Secretly, Stapledon left for Boulogne and England where he immediately informed Edward and the Despensers of the sinister conspiracy being hatched in France.

Greatly alarmed, the King wrote to his Queen, to his son Prince Edward and to Charles IV commanding his wife and son to return to England.[10] To the Prince he wrote:

Edward, Fair Son,
    We have seen by your letters lately written to us, that ye well remember the charges we enjoined you on your departure from Dover and that ye have not transgressed our commands in any point that was in your power to avoid. But to us it appears that you have not fully obeyed our command as a good son ought to his father, since you have not returned to us, to be under government on our blessing but have notoriously held companionship and your mother also, with Mortimer, our traitor and mortal enemy, who in company with your mother and others, was publicly carried to Paris in your train to the solemnity of the coronation, at Pentecost, just past, in signal despite of us, and to the great dishonour both of us and you; for truly he is neither a meet companion for your mother nor for you, and we hold that much evil to the country will come of it. Also we understand that you, through counsel, which is contrary both to our interest and yours, have proceeded to make divers alterations, injunctions and ordnances without our advice and contrary to our orders in the Duchy of Guienne which we have given you...

9

The King was well aware that it was Isabella who was preventing his son from returning to England. "Cease all excuses of your mother," he told him, "and come to us here with all haste, that we may ordain for you and your states as honourably as you desire." In the same letter Edward II strictly ordered his son not to marry without his consent.

Prince Edward might well plead that his mother was preventing his return. Surely, however, now he was aged thirteen he had a mind of his own, knowing full well that he owed a duty to the King his father as well as to his mother. Was he so much under the domination of Isabella and her paramour that he was deprived of the choice to obey his father's wishes? Far more likely that Isabella had taken every opportunity to fill Edward's mind with dislike of his father and loathing of the Despensers, knowing that many of the nobility, fearful of her husband's subjection to the favourites, wanted to get rid of King and minister. One would like to believe that Prince Edward tried hard to persuade his mother that they should return to England, but in France she was so much under her lover's domination that it is likely that she could not visualize her life without him, knowing his fate if ever he were to return.

So, Edward II contrived to write his pitiful letters in vain. "Edward, Fair son," he wrote on March 18th 1326, "Edward, fair son, you are of tender age, take our commandments tenderly to heart, and so rule your conduct with humility, as you would escape our grief and indignation and advance your own interest and honour. Believe no counsel that is contrary to the will of your father as the wise King Solomon instructs you. Understand certainly that if you now act contrary to our counsel and continue in wilful disobedience, you will feel it all the days of your life and all other sons will take example to be disobedient to their lords and fathers."

Edward wrote the Queen in much the same vein. Isabella's excuse for staying on in France was always the same, that she feared for her life. Her hatred of the Despensers knew no bounds. He told his son in another letter that his mother "devises pretences from absenting herself from us on account of our dear and faithful nephew Hugh de Depenser. She openly, notoriously and knowing it to be contrary to her duty and against the welfare of our crown, has attached to herself and retains in her company the Mortimer, our traitor and mortal foe and worse than this can be, in allowing you to consort with our said enemy and you openly to herd and associate with him in the sight of all the world, doing so great a villainy and dishonour both to yourself and us, to the prejudice of our Crown and of the laws and customs of our realm, which you are supremely bound to hold, preserve and maintain". It is unfortunate that Prince Edward's letters to his father, if any, have not been preserved. In one of Isabella's letters to the King she had promised not to keep Edward in France against his will. Nor was Charles IV detaining him "against the form of your safe-conduct".

Edward complained to his brother-in-law of the Queen's misconduct, alleging that she had only feigned friendship with Despenser in several recent letters because "it was expedient for her support in past time not to secure herself from worse treatment she who ought to be the mediatress between us of entire and lasting peace, should not be the cause of stirring up fresh strife, but the thought of her heart was to devise that pretence for withdrawing from us." How bitterly must Edward and the Despensers have rued their fatal mistake in allowing Isabella to leave for France and his son to follow her.

It was Sir Hugh Despenser the Younger, who got wind of the hostile intentions of many noblemen in England, secretly corresponding with Isabella and promising their support. They urged her to come over to England, having mustered a force of 1,000 men. According to Froissart, Despenser sent secret messengers into France "with great plenty of golde and silver and ryche jewells", intended as bribes for Charles IV and his chief nobles.

King Edward complained to the Pope, and wrote a sharp letter to his brother-in-law that "on peyne of cursing he should send his sister Isabella into Englande to the Kinge her husband".

In his *Chronicles* Froissart treats Isabella as an injured wife. He relates that the Queen "secretly dyd purvey to go into

11

France", implying that she was a fugitive when in reality she was charged with a diplomatic mission. Nor does he mention Mortimer in his account of Isabella's nefarious life in France, fearing, perhaps, to embarrass her son Edward III after ascending the throne. As a story teller Froissart keeps his readers spell-bound, but as a historian he is apt to wander from the truth.

By the end of 1325, the adulterous affair between Mortimer and the Queen was the talk of Paris. Even her own brother was so disgusted at the scandal that he told Isabella that she must "avoyde his realme, or else he wolde cause her to avoyde with shame".

There is a scene in Marlowe's *Edward the Second* where the Queen, desperate for advice what course to follow, consults her young son Edward. The Prince says:

> Madam, return to England
> and please my father well
> and then a fig
> For all my uncle's friendship
> here in France.[11]

If Edward ever offered such advice she certainly did not take it.

At this juncture her cousin Sir Robert de Artois secretly visited Isabella by night, a brave action because Charles IV had threatened that anybody speaking to him on her behalf would "leese his landis and he banysshed the realm".[12] Warning her that she was in deadly danger, he advised her to travel to the independent duchy of Heynault (Hainault), whose ruler was Count Guyllaume (William) of Hainault, married to Isabella's first cousin. So the Queen pursued her journey, together with Prince Edward, stopping for one night at Ambreticourt, the seat of Sir Eustace D'Ambreticourt, an impoverished knight. Young lusty knights are usually susceptible to the piteous stories of fair ladies. No sooner had Sir John of Hainault, Count William's younger brother, heard of Queen Isabella's plight than he hastened to her side on horseback, with a small party of men. Isabella, posing as an innocent, injured wife, Sir John

12

was as putty in her hands. He succumbed to the wheedling of a beautiful, evil woman. "Fayre lady," said this soldier of fortune, "behold me here your owne knyght, who shall not fayle you to dye in the quarrell." He was prepared to organize sufficient "men of war" to accompany the Queen and Prince Edward to England. Isabella was very gracious, saying, "Syr, I fynde in you more love and comforte than in all the worlde...and yf ye wyll do this ye have promised...I and my sonne shall be to you for ever bounde and wyll put all the realme of Ingland in your abandon".

They were given a very warm reception by Count William and his Countess Jane de Valois, Isabella's cousin, in Valenciennes their capital. It so happened that William had four comely daughters, Margaret, Philippa, Jane and Isobel. We are told that during their stay of eight days Prince Edward was much attracted to Philippa, seeking her company more than any of her sisters. Edward was now in his fifteenth year and Philippa, a tall girl with a roseate complexion, dark brown eyes and hair, only a few months younger. She certainly shed tears at his departure, fearing for his safety on account of the dangerous enterprise he was about to embark on. The mutual attraction of Edward and Philippa for one another suited Isabella's plans, for she suggested their betrothal to Count William, also a Count of Holland and Zeeland. Deeming it advantageous, Count William agreed to allow her part payment of Philippa's marriage portion. This betrothal had neither the approval nor authority of Prince Edward's father or the Council. For a long time Edward II had been negotiating a possible marriage for his eldest son with the infanta Eleanora of Aragon.

The part payment of Philippa's marriage portion enabled the Queen to raise a small army of Hainaulters,[13] consisting mainly of mercenaries under the command of Sir John of Hainault. The army was commanded by the Queen's paramour Roger Mortimer of Wigmore. What folly on Edward II's part to send Mortimer's legal wife to a convent after her husband's escape from the Tower, instead of providing facilities for her to visit Paris to confront the guilty pair.

Froissart gives a dramatic description of the voyage, how they embarked at Dordrecht when "a tempeste toke them in the sea, that put them so farre out of their course that they wist not of two days wher they were." They landed on 24th September 1326 in the estuary of the Orwell[14] near Harwich on the Suffolk side of the river. From the first, Isabella received powerful support from her husband's half-brothers, Thomas Brotherton Earl of Norfolk and Edmund Earl of Kent, mainly because of their hatred of the Despensers. Another important recruit was Henry of Leicester (younger brother of Earl Thomas of Lancaster). Several bishops quickly joined the Queen's party, the treacherous, subtle Adam of Orleton, the Bishop of Lincoln and others.

Edward II and the Despensers were in the Tower, proclaiming all those who had taken arms against the King as traitors and offering £1,000 for Mortimer's head. Finding that he had no support among the Londoners, Edward and his friends decided to flee to Western England. He had stupidly antagonized the Londoners by blaming them indiscriminately for Mortimer's earlier escape from the Tower. The West was the only part of the kingdom where Edward had a following. The Welsh people loved Edward and it was there that the Despensers had their estates and much local power.

Accompanied by the Earl of Arundel, the elder Hugh, the Despensers' son-in-law, the Chancellor Baldock, the Bishop of Norwich and a few adherents, Edward fled to Bristol.

Meanwhile the Londoners in their fury, believing Isabella's letters posted on the Cross in Cheapside that she was a wronged wife, seized the loyal Treasurer, Walter Stapledon of Exeter, in Cheapside, stripped him naked and barbarously executed him. These were bloody times. The Bishop's head was even later sent the revengeful Queen at Gloucester as a trophy when she thanked the London mayor for his late bloody deed, styling it an excellent piece of justice. It is with a sense of deep horror that one reads about Isabella's cruelty. Did she inherit it from her father Philip IV, an able King? At the later trial of Bishop Orleton of Hereford, it was alleged that he had once preached at Wallingford that Edward II, in a typical Plantagenet rage, had said that if he had no other weapon he would crush his wife with his teeth. He had learnt to loathe her and she certainly now hated and despised him.

For the biographer of Edward III it might seem strange that the young prince forced to witness scenes of horror and violence during the Revolution 1326-27, did not become a complete neurotic. Although his mother would constantly tell him that his father was a pervert, unworthy to rule, it is likely that the prince had a fondness for his father as the wretched King had for him. Behind Isabella was the menacing, ambitious, grim Roger Mortimer. The prince could scarcely have liked his mother's lover, yet felt powerless to oppose him openly. It was no doubt Prince Edward's early marriage to the sensible, shrewd and understanding Philippa - a beneficial influence throughout their long married life - that freed him from neurosis.

Prince Edward's younger brother John of Eltham, a lad of eleven, was in the Tower. After the fortress surrendered to the mob he was firstly handed over to their tender mercies and later to his mother. Meanwhile the Queen's growing army moved westward in hot pursuit of the King and the Despensers. At Oxford, Adam of Orleton, Mortimer's friend, preached a treasonable sermon on the theme 'My head grieveth me, a vaine and slothfull head ought necessarily be taken away from the administration of a kingdom.'[15]

Edward II with the younger Hugh Despenser, after reaching Tintern on the Wye - the lovely Cistercian abbey, which would have been almost two hundred years old by then - fled to Chepstow. There they chartered a boat, intending to sail for Lundy Island in the Bristol Channel, a possession of the Despensers. The winds were unfavourable and they were driven back to Cardiff. There they wandered about Glamorgan, but were betrayed into the hands of Henry Earl of Leicester at Neath Abbey. On November 16th 1326, Edward was brought from Monmouth and Ledbury to Leicester's Castle at Kenilworth, where he remained all winter, though treated by no means unkindly by his cousin.

Meanwhile Bristol had surrendered to Isabella and Mortimer. After his capture Hugh the elder Earl of Winchester,

15

aged sixty-four, then considered an old man, was sentenced to a ghastly death, "to be drawne and hanged in his armour, taken downe alive...his bowels burned and his body cast to hogs to be eaten". These ghastly proceedings were given a temporary pseudo-legality by appointing Prince Edward Duke of Aquitaine, 'Custos (Keeper) of the Realm'. Hugh the younger Despenser and the Earl of Arundel met similar hideous fates at Hereford.

Whether the Westminster Parliament of January 1326 was legally constituted it is difficult to say, for the King was absent, held prisoner in Kenilworth. However, the barons, the majority of the bishops and the people, were determined to depose him and to place on the throne his eldest son, Prince Edward. Even the turncoat, Walter Reynolds Archbishop of Canterbury, deserted his benefactor Edward II, preaching a sermon *vox populi, vox dei*, while Orleton, exulting with a smooth smile on his face, preached a parliamentary sermon, 'A foolish king shall ruin his people'.

At least Prince Edward, barely fourteen, pressed to become King, declared courageously and stubbornly that he could not consent unless his father agreed to renounce his throne. Six Articles of Deposition were read to the assembly.

When a deputation of hostile bishops, including Stratford, Bishop of Winchester, visited Edward II at Kenilworth, attempting to persuade him to attend the proceedings at Westminster, he roundly cursed them as traitors, refusing to comply. However, a second deputation under the leadership of Sir William Trussell, a former follower of Thomas of Lancaster, succeeded in their object. They had to persuade Edward to renounce his crown, and to agree that his eldest son should take his place. For Edward it was a real tragedy. Dressed in a black gown of mourning, grief-stricken, almost bereft of his wits, he came out of his secret chamber, not without a sense of theatre, to hear what amounted to an ultimatum. The crafty Bishop Orleton made sure that Edward had no choice. If the King were to refuse to resign his crown, he threatened, the people might not only repudiate him, but his children also, and choose some

16

fitter man to be their king. Sobbing bitterly, Edward was forced
to agree to their harsh terms.

So Edward of Windsor now Edward III, was proclaimed
King on January 24th 1327,[16] his reign beginning the following
day. A week later he was crowned in Westminster Abbey by
the craven Reynolds, Archbishop of Canterbury. It is said that
his mother Isabella wept throughout the ceremony, but it is unlikely that her tears were genuine. For three years, young
Edward was to some extent under the domination of his
vindictive mother and her evil lover, Roger Mortimer. The new
king was a handsome youth about six foot tall, lacking the
commanding height of his grand-father Edward Longshanks,
who was at least six foot two. John Stow wrote of Edward III:

> This Prince was embued with passing beautie and favour
> of wit, provident, circumspect and gentle of nature, of
> excellent modesty and temperance. He advanced such
> persons to dignities, as did excell other in innocency of
> life.[17]

A new Parliament now reversed the sentence passed on
Edward II's cousin Thomas, Earl of Lancaster, so that Henry of
Leicester, his younger brother, could inherit the title. Both
Isabella "that fierce and cruel" woman (as Stow called her) and
Adam of Orleton considered that Lancaster was treating his
cousin too kindly at Kenilworth. It would seem that he had
taken pity on Edward. It was feared lest his well-wishers might
bring about the escape of "the old King" as Stow describes him,
though he was only forty-three. So new keepers were found for
him, Sir John Maltravers and Sir Thomas Gournay, both sup-
porters of Mortimer and the Queen. They brought the deposed
King firstly to Corfe Castle in Dorset, then to Bristol Castle and
finally to Berkeley Castle nearby, the residence of Sir Thomas
Berkeley, Mortimer's son-in-law.

Joshua Barnes in his *Biography of Edward III*[18] (1686) - the
earliest to be written - gives a harrowing account of the
wretched Edward of Caernarvon's passage to Berkeley Castle,
insulted by the vile Gournay and others. To mock him, they set
on his head a crown made of a wisp of hay. When Edward sat
on a mole-hill to be shaved and to have his beard trimmed,

17

they bought him "cold and dirty water in an old rusty helmet, saying: 'That cold water should serve him for that time', to which the abused former King replied meekly: 'But whether you will allow it or not, I will have warm water for my beard.' Then a shower of warm tears overflowed his face and beard."

The Baker Chronicle (*Chronicon Galfridi le Baker de Swynebroke*) is the original authority for the story that Edward's gaolers gave him meats, often unsavoury, always unwholesome, sometimes tempered with loathsome sauces and even poisons, but his strong constitution preserved him from all their devilish concoctions. He survived even the horror of being shut up in a close chamber, with the constant stench of dead carcases afflicting his senses from a cellar below. The manner of Edward of Caernarvon's murder is somewhat mysterious, though he was almost certainly put to death through the connivance of the evil Mortimer and Queen Isabella. Bishop Orleton is said to have sent an ambiguous letter in Latin to Edward's gaolers. "*Edwardum occidere nolite timere bonum est*", which could be translated: "Do not slay Edward: it is a good thing to be afraid" or alternatively, "Do not fear to slay Edward: it is a good thing", depending on the punctuation. Such a letter seems characteristic of Orleton, with his sly humour, but he was at Avignon at the time of Edward's death, no doubt intriguing to further his career, so it may well be untrue.

Sir Thomas Berkeley was paid one hundred shillings per day for Edward's keep, but he conveniently removed himself to another house, so can only be held morally responsible for what occurred.

No passage in Marlowe's *Edward the Second* is more powerful than the soaring passion with which he described Edward's agonizing death.[19] John Trevisa was vicar of Berkeley during Sir Thomas Berkeley's lifetime, and he relates that Edward was partly smothered, then cruelly killed "with a hoote broche putte thro the secret place posterialle".[20] Officially, of course, it was given out that the deposed King had died a natural death. How many believed it? Men feared for their lives if they pointed the finger of suspicion at Mortimer or the Queen. It is impossible to conceive that Edward III did not suspect that Mortimer was his father's murderer when he heard of his death whilst at Lincoln. He certainly mourned at the news with more sincerity than his mother, who not surprisingly looked very troubled. Did her son suspect her connivance in the affair? It is very probable. He was placed in a terrible quandary, his filial ties of affection for Isabella at war with his natural sense of justice.

We know the fate of several of the murderers. Sir Thomas Gournay was first captured at Burgos, but escaped to Naples, to be arrested eventually by the new King's commissioners. According to the Baker Chronicle, the Murimuth Chronicle and John Stow, he was beheaded at sea, for it was feared that he might accuse various great persons of the crime.[21] Sir John Maltravers seems to have deeply repented of his misdeeds, living a long time in Germany, but later serving Edward III so faithfully in Flanders that he was given, after more than twenty years, a full pardon.[22] As for Sir Thomas Berkeley, he faced prosecution early in the new reign, but after nearly seven years, his plea of ignorance was accepted. He, too, gave Edward III good service in France and Scotland, dying in 1361.

Both mother and son attended the lavish funeral held at the Abbey Church of St.Peter in Gloucester. Who can delve into the mind of Isabella as she stood there that day? What dark thoughts clouded it? She knew, however, what was expected of her, so she yielded to sorrow.

Edward III was but a puppet king for the first three years of his reign, for Mortimer and the Queen Isabella were the real rulers, until Edward staged his *coup d'état* against Mortimer in Nottingham Castle. Then he erected a magnificent tomb to his father's memory - a far from saintly character - in Gloucester Abbey, a place of pilgrimage for thousands of people, who believed that miracles were performed there. It was left to Edward II's great-grandson many years later, the ill-fated Richard II, to try to get his forebear canonized, but he failed to achieve his object.

Froissart, so eloquent on the subject of Queen Isabella, is curiously reticent about her husband. He makes a bare allusion to Edward's death. During September 1366 he was the guest of

Edward Lord Despenser, the grandson of Hugh, Edward's minister at Berkeley Castle. He then discreetly inquired of an old squire what had become of that King, only to be told that they had shortened his life for him.[23]

II Edward Comes Into His Own

The England of 1327, ruled by the tyrant Roger Mortimer, created Earl of March, and his infamous royal mistress, Isabella 'She-wolf' of France, much to the humiliation of the Plantagenet boy king Edward, was a land of virgin and royal forests. There was the New Forest, Savernake, Windsor Forest, Arden and Sherwood. For the traveller to venture abroad was extremely hazardous, since outlaws and robbers haunted the deeply rutted roads. Unbridged streams flowed into low-lying fields. England was then a very sparsely populated country, and one mainly consisting of farmers, fishermen and sheep graziers, an exporter of raw materials and an importer of manufactured goods. The population of the whole country was, perhaps, 4,500,000, while London had a population of a mere 35,000, York 11,500 and other towns only 10,000. Yet England was of growing commercial importance, having dealings with many parts of the continent and fast capturing a massive share of the cloth trade. Wool was the most important export, especially profitable to the King.

London was the political and administrative centre of the kingdom, a noisy town, especially during the law terms and during sessions of parliament, when students, lawyers, clerks and the magnates came there. Despite its squalor there was beauty, the sweet chiming of the bells of St.Mary Archers (Bow Church) warning the chance traveller lest he should be benighted in the fields. Open channels for refuse ran through the streets into streams and ditches, breeding disease. Butchers slaughtered their beasts in Fleet Street.

In contrast, France was the richest and most populous country in Europe, with a population, perhaps, five times greater than England. It resembled England because it was mainly a rural land, but the villages were much larger. So were the towns, such as Bordeaux, Toulouse and Rouen, whose population was about 30,000 people. Great landed aristocrats such as the Dukes of Brittany, Burgundy and Guyenne owned enormous territories. There was a curious link between our Plantagenet kings and the French monarchy in the early fourteenth century, for the former had by no means liberated themselves finally from their French origins. With their French blood, their family relations, language, taste, culture and, above all, their territorial possessions, made them bound closely to France. As already mentioned, England still held part of the old duchy of Aquitaine, the Channel Isles and since 1292 (during Edward I's reign) the county of Ponthieu in Northern France, for which they were obliged to pay homage.

Such was the unhappy land of England ruled by Mortimer and Queen Isabella, hated and feared as much as the Despensers. Mortimer was unscrupulous, insolent, arrogant and even more greedy for land and money than Edward II's favourites. He held the great post of Justice of Wales, but the country was shamefully misgoverned. Mortimer took a sadistic delight in boasting of his power over the adolescent Edward and was surrounded by greater pomp. Wild bands of Welsh mercenaries attended on him, wreaking destruction. However, both Queen and paramour felt the insecurity of the tyrant, forever suspicious and jealous of possible supplanters. According to the contemporary chronicler Galfridi Le Baker de Swynebroke, King Edward was present at Hereford when two of Mortimer's daughters made powerful marriages, Beatrix with Edward, son of Thomas of Brotherton, and Agnes with Laurence, son of Lord Hastings and afterwards Earl of Pembroke.[1]

All the contemporary chroniclers, including the *Brut Chronicle*, have accounts revealing that Edward II's half brother, Edmund of Kent, a rather foolish nobleman, was trapped by Mortimer and the Queen and condemned to death. Edmund had shown bitter remorse for having opposed Edward II, so they sought to destroy him. Rumours were rampant that the late King was not dead, but remained a close prisoner in Corfe Castle. The Earl of Kent, too credulous and superstitious by nature, was told by a friar that he had seen the deposed King at a

22

distance. He then wrote a warm letter to his half-brother, but it fell into Mortimer's hands. Edward III was now attending his parliament at Winchester, and it is evident according to the *Brut Chronicle* that Isabella did her best to arouse her son's feelings against his uncle, "and bade him, uppon hire benysoun that he shulde ben avengede uppon him, as uppon his dedely enemy". Edmund of Woodstock was arrested and accused of high treason against the young King.[2] It seems probable that Edward would have liked to save his uncle's life, but he was powerless against the combined onslaught of his mother and Mortimer. Edmund was executed at Winchester. Mortimer now added to his retinue, having as many as one hundred and eighty knights in his establishment.

Edward III was aged fifteen when he took part in his first campaign against Scotland, but it was hardly a success. He had lately confirmed the truce made by his father with Scotland, but Robert the Bruce, the victor of Bannockburn, a great king, had broken the truce, though provoked to do so. He complained that Englishmen had committed various acts of piracy against Scottish shipping and his grievances had gone unheeded. Robert I was now fifty-two, quite old in that age and smitten with leprosy or a like disease. Taking advantage of the troubles in England, he issued a challenge to Edward III, threatening to invade the country, ravage and burn it as far southward as he had done earlier when he had defeated the English at Stirling Castle.

Froissart's account is largely based on Jean Le Bel's *Chronique*, particularly valuable because he served through the campaign in the company of John of Hainault (Lord of Beaumont), his patron. Le Bel was born at Liège about 1290, being descended from an old family called 'Del Cange' and eventually became Canon of Liège. For Edward III throughout his reign, Le Bel had the greatest of admiration, usually referring to him as noble and skilled (*preux*) and comparing him favourably with Philip VI of France. Though much less colourful than Froissart, Le Bel, as an historian, adheres more strictly to the truth. He is sensitive to nature, describing Northumberland as 'sauvage pays, plain (plein) de deserts et de grands montagnes'.

He is not without pity or without heart, but he shows little sympathy for the drowning English in the River Tyne when in pursuit of the Scots. Perhaps one of the most moving passages is his account of the last moments of King Robert Bruce recommending his young heir, David, to his lords (1329).

Edward III organized a large army against the Scots, sending an urgent message to Sir John of Hainault asking for succour. The lusty knight had recently returned to Valenciennes, richly rewarded with money and jewels for his part in siding with the Queen and Mortimer against the deposed King. According to the *Chronicon* of Galfridi Le Baker[3], John of Hainault already held a pension of 1,000 marks, granted by Edward III, February 7th 1327. In March 1328, the King stipulated to pay him as much as £74,406.6s.9d. in two instalments, for twice coming to his assistance. Besides native troops, John of Hainault provided 2,500 German cavalry to fight with Edward's army.

Edward arrived in York towards the end of May, to be joined by the Hainaulters.

Le Bel and the other contemporary chroniclers describe the serious dissension and quarrels that broke out between the English archers and the *seigneurs* in the entourage of John of Hainault on Trinity Sunday in York. He calls it a riot, resulting in a fight between the foreigners and the English archers owing to a quarrel over dice. *The Eulogium Historiarum* by a monk of Malmesbury, agrees with Baker in describing the fight between the Hainaulters and the citizens of York.[4] Eventually the archers were repulsed with the loss of three hundred. Le Bel relates that the young King ordered an inquiry into the reasons for the outbreak. Froissart thought that the affray was instigated by the friends of the Despensers wanting to be revenged on John of Hainault for having been a party to their execution. Froissart, a Hainaulter, lavishly praises his compatriot Sir John. "I trowe God dyd never gyve more grace and fortune to any people than he dyd as than to this gentle knyght, Sir John of Heynault and to his companye." He indignantly blames the English archers for wanting to murder and rob the Hainaulters, "for all they were come to serve the Kyn in his besynesse". Perhaps the cause of the riot was the xenophobia of the English.

Young King Edward and his troops experienced much hardship on this campaign. On one occasion at least his life was in jeopardy when James Douglas, one of the commanders of the Scots, a grand fighter (the commander-in-chief was the Earl of Moray), followed by 200 carefully selected horsemen, managed to penetrate the English lines at midnight. As he rode furiously "straking his horse with the spurres, Douglas cried: 'Duglas, Duglas, ye shall all dye, thieves of England'."[5] Froissart relates that he actually reached "the Kyngis (King's) own tent and strake a sundre 11 or 111 cordis of the Kyngis tent", and so departed, losing some of his men when retreating. Edward might easily have been slain had it not been for the devotion of his chaplain and his attendants, who sacrificed their lives to save him.

Edward's later campaigns in France and Scotland are so replete with glory and glamour that his first campaign certainly caused him sore disappointment. We see the boy king being brought forward on horseback by his lords to make a speech to his army, intending to give them courage. He was gracious and majestic, even in boyhood. "The King in full goodly maner prayed and requyred them ryght graciously that every man wolde payne them to do theyr beste, to save his honour and common weale of his realme."[6] Later Edward was to acquire the magnetism of a born leader of men.

Perhaps the most valuable picture provided by Froissart was his description of the light cavalry of the army of the Scots on this expedition: "These Scots are right handy, and sore travelyng in harney (harness), and in warres"[7] he wrote. "When they make their invasions into England, they marched from 20 to 24 miles without halting, as well by night as by day; for they were all on horse-back, except the camp-followers, who were on foot. The knights and squires are well mounted on large bay horses, the common people on little nags. They bring no carriages with them on account of the mountains they have to pass in Northumberland; neither do they carry with them any provisions of bread or wine, for their habits of sobriety are such in time of war that they will live for a long time on flesh, half-sodden, without bread, and drink the river water without wine. They have therefore no occasion for pots and pans, for they dress the flesh of their cattle in the skins after they have taken them off,...This army was commanded by two valiant captains. The King of Scotland himself (Robert the Bruce), who had been very brave, yet being old and labouring under a leprosy ('sore grieved with the great sickeries') appointed for one that gallant prince, so renowned in arms, the Earl of Moray ...the other the Lord James (Froissart calls him erroneously William) Douglas, esteemed the bravest and most enterprising knight in the two kingdoms.[8] The Scots, in later years, derided their hereditary enemies, nicknaming them as "pock-puddings". Holinshed recorded that the English soldiers were "cloathed all in cotes and hoods embroidered with floures and branches verie seemlie, and used to nourish their beards". These gaudy coats contrasted with the austere garments worn by the hardy Scots.

Despite many feats of valour on the part of English and Scots, it is fair to say the Edward's army was outgeneralled. The failure of the young king's first campaign cannot be blamed on Roger Mortimer, who was accused of having taken a bribe of £20,000 from the Scots, though later charged with having embezzled money paid by them and stipulated under the Treaty of Northampton (1328).

Despite being heavily outnumbered, the Scots were very nimble at outwitting their more powerful enemy.

Edward's army was disbanded at York on August 15th. John of Hainault's heavy cavalry had been a costly expense, for many of the war-horses had died owing to the severe climate in Scotland. To replenish them, more horses had to be bought in York. According to Froissart, Sir John of Hainault and his company were "greatly feasted by the Quene (Isabella) and all other ladyes" in York. The King moved to Durham where he took up his quarters in the great courtyard of an abbey, proceeding the following day to Durham Cathedral with his nobles. There the bishop and chapter together with the citizens took the oath of fealty to him for the first time.

The preliminary negotiations for a peace between the two countries, much to the advantage of Scotland and representing a triumph for Robert the Bruce, were settled at a Parliament held at York (March 1st 1328). The terms were ironically enough that there should be perpetual peace between England and Scotland, that David Bruce (Robert's son) should marry the infant Joan of the Tower, aged seven, Edward III's sister, that all deeds relating to the subjection of Scotland to England and the famous Stone of Scone should be surrendered.

This Stone had been removed to Westminster by Edward III's grandfather in 1296. The young king now issued a writ to the Dean and Chapter of Westminster ordering them to hand it over on July 1st 1328 to the Sheriffs of London, who were to bear it to Queen Isabella, but the Abbot of Westminster, William de Curtlyngton, supported by the citizens of London, refused to part with it.[9] By the Treaty, Robert Bruce had to pay 30,000 marks (£20,000) to the King of England at the rate of 10,000 marks annually on the anniversary of the Battle of Bannockburn.

This clause was imposed to make reparation for the ravages committed by the Scots in England. Le Baker described this treaty as a *"turpis pax"* (disgraceful peace), and the English felt humiliated and considered it shameful.

Edward III greatly admired his grandfather Edward I as a great warrior. The young Edward, was almost six foot in height, well and gracefully made, brave, strong, possessing the dignity his father lacked, godlike, his eyes blue, he wore a short beard, and his hair was neither red nor yellow, but a fair mixture of silver and gold.[10] Edward's violent temper, however, was greatly feared by his contemporaries, though all the Plantagenets were passionate by nature. He never sulked. His charm was such that he could win back his friends if he had hurt them. The only person capable of mitigating Edward's fits of anger was Philippa, the girl he was soon to marry.

Philippa was the early patron of her compatriot Jean Froissart, and would relate to him, after she became Queen of England, her recollection of those sweet, brief days in Valenciennes when Prince Edward had inclined with eyes of love to her rather than to her sisters. When asked as King whether he intended to adhere to his betrothal, he laughed merrily, saying, "Yes, I am better pleased to marry there than elsewhere and rather to Philippa, for she and I accorded excellently well together, and she wept, I know well, when I took leave of her at my departure." As the mothers of Edward and his betrothed were cousins-german, it was necessary to obtain a dispensation from the Pope at Avignon. Orleton, now Treasurer, was charged with this mission.

After many formalities, Philippa, escorted by her uncle John of Hainault Lord Beaumont, landed at Dover in late December 1327. In London, she was given a magnificent reception, being presented by the Mayor and Aldermen with a service of plate worth £300 as a wedding gift.[11] Froissart relates: "And ther was also great justes, tourneys, dancing, carolying and great feastis every day; the whiche endured the space of 111 weekis". She was always to remain popular in England. During January 1328 Edward sojourned in the north, engrossed in affairs of state dealing with Scotland, so Philippa set off on her journey to York, a slow, arduous one, owing to the inclement season and bad state of the roads.

Edward and Philippa were united in marriage on January 24th 1328, the eve of the Conversion of St. Paul in York Minster. No event in the King's dramatic life was more fortunate, for she was to make him a splendid Queen, accompanying him on his campaigns, and never wavering from her fidelity to him, despite Edward's shortcomings as a faithful husband. England, too, prospered when the King came into his own, but only so long as Philippa lived. In his account of their wedding, Froissart first mentions Watetet (Walter) of Manny, a fellow Hainaulter, who probably first came to England in Philippa's train before her marriage and remained in her service. He is alluded to as "her karver" and became one of her squires. He was knighted in 1331, and as a soldier of fortune rendered Edward III long and distinguished service in France and Scotland. Except for Manny, few of Queen Philippa's attendants remained with her. After the final peace with Scotland, the royal couple during the spring (1328) returned slowly

28

southward from Lincoln to Northampton and then to Oxford-shire, where they stayed in the royal palace of Woodstock. It became Philippa's favourite palace.

Since the Queen-Mother Isabella had already spent Philippa's portion, the King promised that £15,000 per annum of lands should be settled on her. We get no indication of the relations between Isabella and her daughter-in-law, though one suspects bearing in mind their widely divergent characters, that they bore each other little real affection. On the other hand, Isabella seems to have encouraged her son's marriage and put no obstacle in its way. Philippa was to become very attached to the Abbey Church of Westminster, and her coronation took place there in 1330. From his palace at Eltham, Edward ordered

> his beloved and faithful Bartholomew de Burgersh to appear with his barons of the Cinque-ports to do their customary duties at the Coronation of his dearest Queen Philippa, which takes place, if God is propitious, the Sunday next to the feast of St. Peter in the Cathedral of Westminster.

Edward's position as a young king was no doubt strengthened by the birth of an infant prince to his Queen at Woodstock on June 15th 1330. He was destined to become the greatest warrior of his age, the illustrious Black Prince, but in his early life he was known as Edward of Woodstock or later Prince of Wales, after his creation by his father. It is curious that Edward III was never created Prince of Wales. Whether Philippa suckled her first-born is by no means clear, but he certainly had a nursemaid.

Growing in confidence, Edward III now became more determined that the hateful rule of Roger Mortimer and the Queen-Mother must end. The problem was to know the right moment to strike.

During a splendid tournament, however, held in Cheap-side between Wood Street and Queen Street, to celebrate the birth of Edward's heir, some carpenters had constructed a temporary tower and accommodation for the Queen and her ladies with insufficient care. When the Queen's party entered the tower, the faultily constructed scaffolding completely gave way. Amidst scenes of terror, Philippa and her ladies fell to the ground. Mercifully, nobody was killed, but Edward had seen what had happened. In one of his uncontrollable fits of passion, he cried that the careless carpenters must immediately be put to death. If it had not been for Queen Philippa throwing herself on her knees before her husband and gently imploring him to pardon the wretched men, it is probable that the King's orders would have been carried out. Other occasions are recorded when she acted in a similar way when Edward gave rein to his anger.

When Parliament met at Nottingham during October 1330, a rumour was sweeping the town that Roger Mortimer was trying every artifice to destroy the King and to usurp his throne. Galfridi Le Baker describes the scene with keen insight, showing that Mortimer intended to destroy those nearest King Edward as well. "He greatly rebuked the King's cousin, the earl of Lancaster, for without his consent he appointed certain lodgings for noblemen in the town, demanding who made him so bold, to take up lodgings so nigh unto the Queen."[12] So Lancaster was forced to move a full mile outside Nottingham. Another nobleman to feel the lash of Mortimer's tongue was John de Bohun, Earl of Hereford, High Constable of England.

The hour was ripe for the young king to have Mortimer arrested, but he wanted firstly to gain the Pope's acquiescence. One of his most intimate friends was William Montagu, who now travelled to Rome for this purpose. On his return, Edward's tutor Bury, Keeper of the Privy Seal, sent the Pope a code-signal *pater sancte* to signify which future communications came from the King himself as opposed to letters drafted by Isabella and her lover.

It was essential for the King and his friends to have as their ally Robert de Holland, longtime seneschal of the Castle, for he knew all the secret passages in its vicinity and secret corners in Nottingham Castle. The enterprise was all the more dangerous because Queen Isabella took the precaution every night of having the keys brought to her, and placed under the pillow in her bed-chamber. Meanwhile, Mortimer, well served by his spies, was aware of the conspiracy against him.

30

Let Stow take up the story.

> Then upon a certain night, the King lying without the Castle, both him and his friends were brought by torchlight through a secret way underground (still known as Mortimer's Hole)...till they came even to the Queen's chamber, which they found by chance open. They therefore being armed with naked swords in their hands, went forwards leaving the King also armed without the doors of the chamber, least his mother should espy him.[13]

Mortimer had been in conference with his advisers and was just about to go to bed with Isabella when there was the clash of steel, as Sir Hugh Turpington, one of Mortimer's friends, resisted the royal invaders. He was killed, and John Neville mortally wounded, being pierced by a sword.

Mortimer was arrested and taken to the hall, while Queen Isabella's cry echoes down the centuries: "Bel filz, bel filz ayez pitie de gentil Mortimer", "good sonne, good sonne, take pity upon gentle Mortimer", for she sensed as a mother that her son was there, though she saw him not. History does not record that anybody other than Isabella ever thought him gentle. The keys of the Castle were immediately surrendered to the King.

Then early on the following morning, a horrid cry was raised indicating the extreme joy of the nobility and common people as Mortimer, with two of his friends, Sir Simon Burford and Sir John Deverel, were taken to London to the Tower for a few hours and afterwards arraigned by his peers in Westminster in the King's presence. Edward demanded of his council what should be done with Mortimer after he had been accused of various crimes. The main accusations were that he had stirred up dissension between Edward II and the Queen. Having usurped the powers of the Council of Regency, he had taught Edward III to regard his cousin Henry of Lancaster as his enemy, and had deluded Edmund Earl of Kent, making him believe that his half-brother was still alive, so procuring his execution. There was no trial. When asked by the King what should be done to Mortimer, his council unanimously told Edward, "Syr, he hath deserved to dye the same dethe that Sir

Hewe Spenser dyed." Mortimer was hanged on the common gallows at the Elms, now known as Tyburn, on November 30th 1330, and the King commanded that his body should hang there for two days and two nights. It was then taken down and buried in the Grey Friar's Church within Newgate.

The young king acted wisely when, at the age of eighteen, he took the reins of government into his hands. He issued writs to the judges, ordering them to administer justice boldly and impartially, without respect of persons or regard of arbitrary orders. During the rule of Mortimer and Queen Isabella, England had been overrun by robbers and murderers, sometimes under the protection of important magnates. The King now made his powerful and lawless barons give their solemn promise that they would no longer give these criminals their protection. A beneficial Act passed in Edward III's early reign was the Statute of Winchester (1331), confirming that each neighbourhood must be responsible for crimes committed there. 'Courts of Traylbaston' (in old French it means 'drawing the stick') were instituted to suppress club law, superseded in 1347 by the establishment of 'Keepers of the Peace', and fourteen years later by 'Justices of the Peace' as they are still called.[14]

Froissart, probably to spare Edward III's feelings, is on the whole reticent about Queen Isabella, though he does mention that it was reported that she was with child by Mortimer.[15] Whatever sentiments Edward now felt for his mother, he could not forget the close tie between them. It would seem that Pope John XXII wrote to Edward exhorting him not to expose Isabella's shame. There could be no public trial. Too many people in high places would be embarrassed. Certainly Edward behaved magnanimously to her, believing that her crimes were mainly due to the dominating influence of her lover. Edward allowed her to go into retirement to Castle Rising in Norfolk with an allowance of £3,000 per annum. Her movements were restricted. Froissart wrote that "she had with her ladyes and damosels, knyghtes and squiers, to serve her according to her estat; and certayne landes assigned to her, to mentayne therewith her noble estat all dayes of her life." Bearing in mind her violent attachment to Mortimer, however, she cannot have relished the appointment of Sir John de Molins as Steward of her household, for he was the first to seize Mortimer in Nottingham Castle. Isabella has been described as a virtual prisoner, but this is not true. She occasionally sallied forth to see some sports in the grounds.

Let us leave her alone with her secrets and her conscience to haunt her. Edward would visit his mother once or twice a year, and we know that later in her life, in 1344, she occasionally attended a great feast at her son's court at Windsor. She was to live for another twenty-eight years, dying in 1358, to be buried in the Franciscan Church at Newgate.

On February 1st 1328 there died at the Castle of Vincennes near Paris, Charles IV, the last Capetian King of France, the only surviving brother of Queen Isabella. By the Salic law of France, no woman could succeed to the throne of France, but it was argued by Edward's proctors, and there was some justification for their case, that his mother could transmit her rights to her son. Edward III was the nearest male heir to the late king, being his nephew, while Philip of Valois was only Charles's first cousin. However the great assembly appointed Philip of Valois regent, and he was soon acknowledged King Philip VI.

It is clear that the French would never have accepted Isabella as Queen of France. They had seen too much or her in Paris, indulging in her notorious love affair with Roger Mortimer. Edward, too, was only fifteen in 1328, and under the domination of his mother and her odious paramour. He was clearly a far less suitable candidate as King of France than Philip of Valois, then aged thirty-five, a tall, handsome nobleman, magnificent in his tastes and famed for his gallantry in the tournament and on the battlefield.[1] He was very superstitious.

During the first few years of his reign, Edward was far too weak to challenge Philip, since he was a puppet king ruling a divided kingdom. However, he assumed real kingship towards the end of 1330. He was obliged and according to Froissart, travelled to Amiens in 1329, to do homage for the Duchy of Guyenne or Aquitaine, held by Kings of England since 1153 (reign of Henry II) as a fief under the French Crown. Edward was received by King Philip with all due honour and dignity. On this occasion, the King of England paid homage with words and a mass only, refusing to go further on the advice of his ministers, until he could return home to consult the earlier documents providing information what form his homage should take. Whilst in France, Edward also paid homage for his county of Ponthieu, at the mouth of the Somme. Relations between the two kings seemed amicable enough, since Edward tarried at Amiens, to be splendidly feasted and entertained. Froissart gives Philip's actual words:

> Cosyn, we woll not disceyve you: this that ye have done pleaseth us right well, as for this present tyme, tyll such tyme as ye be returned agayne into your realme and that ye have sene under the seales of you predecessours, howe, and in what wyse ye should do.

However, after a study of the documents when he returned to England, it was clear that Edward had to pay liege homage without reservation for the fiefs of Aquitaine, Ponthieu and Montreuil.

From 1333 Edward was fully occupied with national reconstruction and unity at home, with less time to deal with affairs overseas. Unlike his father, he showed an instinctive flair for handling the great men of the realm. He was magnanimous in his treatment of the Mortimer faction, reluctantly promoting Orleton to the bishopric of Winchester in 1333, for he did not like him and sent him on an embassy to France. Another of Mortimer's men, Bishop Burghersh, appointed Treasurer in 1334, was the uncle of Bartholomew, later an intimate friend of Edward's. Nor did the young king neglect his friends, bestowing a peerage on William Montagu in 1331 and later creating him Earl of Salisbury. His cousin Henry of Grosmont, son of the Earl of Lancaster, he created Earl of Derby, later a great soldier, and Robert d'Ufford became Steward of the household and Earl of Suffolk. The older nobility, the Fitzalans, the Beauchamps and the Bohuns all prospered during Edward's reign.

The most influential of Edward III's ministers during his early reign was John de Stratford, born at Stratford-on-Avon and educated at Merton College, Oxford. In his earlier career he had been consecrated Bishop of Winchester by the Cardinal Bishop of Albano during 1323, but Edward II had dismissed him from office, though he was later restored to favour. Bishop Stubbs the historian approved of him, describing him "as something of a statesman", and it is true that he was more of a politician than an ecclesiastic, too much absorbed in worldly affairs. Stratford, however, took a leading part in drawing up the six articles of Deposition against Edward III's father, and was one of the bishops sent to Kenilworth Castle to obtain his formal abdication, according to Baker's Chronicle. Fearless by nature, he soon incurred the enmity of Mortimer, who would have liked to have put him to death. Edward III wisely appointed him Chancellor and he was to remain the young king's chief adviser until 1340. Although he was fond of Edward, Stratford was no mealy-mouthed sycophant. Later he showed considerable courage when they engaged in a bitter quarrel. It was customary, in that age, for prelates to negotiate the marriages of princesses of the blood royal, and Stratford went to France to negotiate that of the King's sister Eleanor and the Count of Gueldres (1332). He had been created archbishop of Canterbury in 1333.

During his early kingship after 1330, Edward revealed real ability and dynamic energy. These were his formative years when his military reputation greatly increased after the brilliant victory of Halidon Hill. However, to understand Edward's policy towards the Scots, it is essential to bear in mind that the King, as a youth of sixteen, was always strongly opposed to the Treaty of Northampton (1328). This shameful peace had been made against his wishes.[2] It was said that Edward had accepted the treaty under compulsion and had testified so before a notary. To show his disapproval he had ostentatiously absented himself when his sister Joan, a mere child, married David Bruce (born at Dunfermline March 24th 1324), not even providing a dowry for her, perhaps intended as an insult to King Robert Bruce, David's father. When his elder sister married the Count of Gueldres, she brought a dowry of £10,000.

When David succeeded his father King Robert in 1329, his rival, Edward Balliol, claimed to be the real King of Scotland, a claim supported by many English and Scots. The dynastic question was of vital importance, in the first part of the fourteenth century, because Edward I in 1292 had awarded the

36

crown of Scotland to John Balliol, Edward's father, only to depose him four years later. There then followed an unsettled period until Robert Bruce, a consummate statesman, became King of Scotland. By the 1330s Edward Balliol, a more forceful character than his father, was challenging David Bruce's inheritance.

Edward III pursued a very devious policy, sometimes favouring the pretender to the throne Edward Balliol, who was willing to acknowledge English suzerainty and sometimes seeking to re-establish English paramountcy through his infant brother-in-law David II of Scotland.

By 1333, the peace provided by the Treaty of Northampton was proving illusory. The King was now openly favouring Edward Balliol's restoration, and giving permission to his subjects to join his expedition. About the second week in March, Balliol and his men, having ravaged the neighbouring countryside, laid siege by land and sea to the town of Berwick and its castle. Berwick on Tweed, because of its commanding border position and massive castle, was a constant object of acquisition in war. Edward's grandfather, 'the hammer of the Scots', had acquired it in 1296, but Robert Bruce had eventually recovered it. Now fifteen years later, the governor of Berwick Castle was Patrick of Dunbar, Earl of March, and its warder Sir Alexander Seton.

In attempting to justify his invasion of Scotland, Edward III was a skilled propagandist, insisting that the Scots had provoked him by their murders, raids and other crimes. When Edward besieged Berwick Castle and its town, it had already been under siege for two months. To achieve his purpose and to compel the defenders of Berwick to surrender, the Chronicle of the Brut relates "that the besiegers made many assaultes with gonnes and with othere engynes to the towne, wherwith thai destroiede many a fair hous, and cherches also were betenadowne into the erthe, with great stones, and spitouse comyng out of gonnes and of other gynnes." It seems probable that firearms were used, for the Scottish chronicler Barbour mentions their use during Edward's first campaign in Scotland.

While her husband was besieging Berwick, Queen Philippa was in Bamburgh Castle, fifteen miles away along the coast. Wishing to apply pressure on the King to abandon his deadly grip on Berwick, Sir Archibald Douglas, the commander of the Scots, instead of laying waste most of Northumberland, laid siege to Bamburgh Castle. Evidently he thought that Edward, fearing for Philippa's safety, would loosen his hold on Berwick, but he was mistaken, for the King knew that Bamburgh possessed sufficient resources to hold out for several weeks.

His treatment of the hostages at Berwick, particularly his harshness towards Thomas, the leading hostage, son of Sir Alexander Seton, amounting to deliberate cruelty,[3] was probably owing to his anxiety and resentment lest his wife should come to any harm. Although Sir Alexander had already lost one son fighting against Balliol and another, William, in the defence of Berwick, he was present when Thomas Seton was hanged. In the circumstances, it seems all the more surprising that, within a month, Sir Alexander Seton became reconciled with the English, being rewarded by Edward with 20 quarters of wheat.[4] However, it was dangerous to defy Edward III and the *Brut* chronicler tells us that the King gave orders "every day for to take 15 hostages of the toune till thai were alle done unto the deth".[5] They had to learn their lesson.

Edward III would later become the beau ideal of chivalry, but we must see him against the background of the fourteenth century, loved and admired by his friends for his charisma and boyish charm, and feared, though respected, by his enemies for being hard-hearted. Yet both his father and grandfather had been accused of cruelty in their dealings with the Scots. One of the charges brought against his father during the deposition proceedings, when Prince of Wales, just before his accession, was his excessive cruelty at the battle of Methven (1306), (Perth).

The battle of Halidon Hill was fought on the eve of St. Margaret's day, July 19th 1333. Edward's army included 1,500 mounted infantrymen and over 15,000 footmen, the majority of whom were archers. It is curious that there were also many volunteers, murderers, robbers and petty criminals, who joined the army to escape being hung, hoping no doubt to obtain a pardon for their crimes.[6] Widespread desertion was a problem in medieval battles, and Edward was clearly troubled by it.

Halidon Hill, five hundred feet high, dominates the approaches to the town of Berwick, for it is distant two miles. It was here in a well-chosen, strategic position that Edward, with the instinctive sense of a born soldier, stationed his troops. The English army was composed of three divisions, the first commanded by the Earl Marshal Brotherton and the Constable, Sir Edward Bohun, the centre by the young King himself, now aged twenty-one, and the third division by Edward Balliol. Each division was largely composed of archers, who played a vital part in the ensuing victory, but men-of-arms also composed Edward's army. Galfridi Le Baker thought it curious that Edward III, together with the other magnates, should fight on foot, contrary to the usual traditions of knightly warfare. The horses were sent to the rear, ready to be used to pursue the enemy.

The army of the Scots was commanded by Sir Archibald Douglas, and contained many footmen in their ranks, each man armed with a pike. Like the English army, the men-of-arms fought dismounted.

Baker gives an entertaining account of how the battle of Halidon was preceded by a single combat fought within view of both armies. A giant Scot named Turnbull contemptuously challenged a Norfolk knight, Robert Venhale, to fight with him.[7]

> At length one Robert Venale, Knight, a Norfolke man, requesting license of the King, being armed with his sword drawne, marcheth towards the champion, meeting by the way a certaine blacke mastiffe dogge, which waited on the champion, whom with his sword he sudanily strake and cut off at his loynes; at the sight whereof the master of the dogge slaine was much abashed, and in his battell more warie and fearefull; whose left hand and head also afterwards this worthy Knight cut off.

Later, Sir Robert de Venhale had a most distinguished career in the foreign campaigns, being summoned to Parliament as baron in 1360.

As the Scots struggled to wade through a treacherous bog to come to grips with the English, they were met by a flight of arrows "as thick as notes on the Sonne berne".[8] The casualties of the Scots were very heavy, for five hundred of their bravest soldiers were killed on the slope of Halidon, known locally as 'Heavyside'. In a gallant fight with Balliol's troops, the first Scottish division, under the young Earl of Moray, was overwhelmed. Losing heart, the remaining Scottish divisions were put to flight. However, some Scots, inspired by the heroism of Hugh, the Earl of Ross, resisted for some time longer, but were almost all killed. The chronicler, Baker, estimated the losses of the Scots exceeding 60,000 killed, while the English casualties were very light.[9] However, the chroniclers vary as to their number. Among those slaughtered were Sir Archibald Douglas their commander, Hugh the gallant Earl of Ross, and other prominent noblemen. After being put to flight, the Scots were pursued by Edward III and his knights, and mostly killed. Medieval warfare was a bloody affair.

When the Meaux chronicler relates that on the morrow of the battle, Edward ordered that a hundred prisoners should be beheaded, it is only fair to mention that the Bridlington Chronicle maintains that before the battle, Sir Alexander Douglas had commanded his men to give no ransom to the enemy.

Edward's triumph at Halidon marked the end of Scottish independence, so laboriously pursued by Robert Bruce. If Edward could have solved the Scottish question, his reputation as a statesman would have been greatly enhanced, but he failed, like his grandfather, a finer statesman. The resilience and powers of endurance of the Scots were to continue troubling Edward III for many a long year. In the meantime, the King could glory in his victory over the hereditary enemy, for the immediate repercussion after the battle was the surrender of Berwick Castle and town to the invading army. The Scots were now forced to stomach the humiliation of seeing their proudest provinces and their strongest fortresses, Edinburgh,

Dunbar, Roxburgh and the whole kingdom south of the Forth, yielded to the enemy. In England, people rejoiced that Bannockburn had been avenged. Although the Scottish Parliament was now obliged to acknowledge Balliol as King of Scotland and to swear allegiance to him, they deeply resented him in their hearts, knowing that he was Edward's creature, a puppet king.

As for the nine year old David II and Joan his wife, they firstly found refuge at Dunbarton after the battle, one of the fortresses bravely resisting under its courageous governor, Malcolm Fleming.[10] Philip VI of France, openly siding with Scotland, now sent him a ship in which David, together with Joan, escaped to Boulogne (May 9th 1334). To further embarrass Edward and his ally, Balliol, Philip gave the royal exiles a splendid reception in Paris, generously installing them in the Château Gallard, a castle built by Richard Coeur de Lion on the Seine near Andelys. David, however, was to develop into a weak, irresolute character, quite unlike his father. He was to reside in France from 1334 until his return to Scotland in 1341. Philip's championship of David, Edward's brother-in-law, certainly did nothing to endear him to the King of England. When Philip announced that any future negotiations between himself and the English must take into consideration the interests of the King of Scots, Edward was very angry.

We last saw his Queen Philippa in Bamburgh Castle, besieged by the Scots. No Queen Consort of England, with the exception of Eleanor of Castile, Edward I's first Queen, showed greater devotion in accompanying her husband on his expeditions. Philippa possessed a strong personality. Intending to welcome Edward, she travelled from York to Durham, planning to spend the night with him in his lodging in St. Cuthbert's Priory near the castle. An amusing story is told of her. She was in her night-gown when a monk timidly knocked at her bedchamber, informing her that it was against the rules of St. Cuthbert for a lady, however high her rank, to sleep within the walls of the convent. Deeply embarrassed, Philippa was obliged to leave hurriedly and spend the night alone in the neighbouring Durham Castle.[11]

Prior to this, she had given birth two years earlier, to her eldest daughter Isabella at the Palace of Woodstock in Oxfordshire (February 5th 1334). Edward doted on Isabella, spoiling his favourite daughter far too much. While the King was on his third northern campaign, Philippa gave birth to her second son, William of Hatfield, born in a village in Yorkshire during the winter (1336). Sadly, he was to survive only a few weeks.

Edward's younger brother, John of Eltham, is rather a shadowy character. When very young, he acted as regent for his brother during Edward's absence in France to do homage for Aquitaine and he was regent on two other occasions when Edward was overseas. In his relations with the Scots, it is unlikely that he was less cruel than his elder brother or his father, but the unconfirmed story that he burnt the church of Lesinchogo in Perthshire with a thousand Scots inside, is almost certainly untrue. He fought at Halidon Hill, and later became a warder of the Marches of Northumberland. As Earl of Cornwall he received a grant of the coinage of tin in Cornwall during April 1336, dying at Perth in the same year, aged twenty. His elaborate medieval tomb in the St. Edmund's Chapel, Westminster Abbey, is beautiful, for the alabaster effigy is one of the first masterpieces of the Nottingham alabasterers and may well be by the same sculptor as the tomb of his father in Gloucester Cathedral.

During the early 1330s Edward tried to negotiate a durable settlement of the Guyenne question with Philip, rather than to go to war with him, but he did not succeed in regaining the Agenais. Nor did Philip show any real hostility to the King of England. Indeed both Edward and Philip planned to go on a crusade together in 1332, a project which received much encouragement from the Pope. Gradually and inexorably, however, relations worsened between them. From 1336 onwards, Philip VI deeply resented the excessive favour Edward showed to Philip's brother-in-law, Robert of Artois. Froissart wrote that Robert had formerly greatly aided Philip to attain to the crown of France, "being one of the most sagest, and greatteste lordes in France". He became a favourite companion in all his enterprises. "All that was done in the realme of France, was done by his advyce." Philip's "mervailouse great displeasure" against Robert was occasioned by his trying to gain possession of Artois, though by law it belonged to his aunt. Not only did he forge documents, but he was accused of witchcraft, suspected of poisoning her when she died.[12] He was tried for murder, condemned to death, and having fallen foul of Philip, "chased out of the realm of France", as Froissart wrote.

Edward created Robert of Artois Earl of Richmond, even giving him a pension and several castles, despite Philip's threat that he considered his enemy anybody who sheltered Robert. Knowing the names of disaffected noblemen in France, Edward found him a useful source of information.

On May 24th 1337, war seemed inevitable, for King Philip then declared that Guyenne had been forfeited by Edward "because of the many excesses, rebellions and disobedient acts committed by the King of England against us and Our Royal Majesty". One of the disobedient acts most resented was the harbouring of Robert of Artois. This declaration marks the beginning of the gigantic conflict between England and France and other powers known as the Hundred Years' War. Edward now retaliated, formally challenging "Philip of Valois who calls himself King of France". He now himself laid claim to the throne of France, at the same time seizing French property in England.

IV Edward Goes To War

'The Hundred Years' War', including periods of truce, was to last from 1337-1456, until the middle of the reign of Henry VI, but the phrase may have been used for the first time about 1850. The causes for the outbreak were complex, not only lying in the disputed succession, but in the manner England and France were developing.[1]

The subject has fascinated many historians. We are familiar with the classic work of Edouard Perroy, and the more recent books by Kenneth Fowler and Desmond Seward. I therefore hasten to say that my biography of Edward III is not intended as another history of the Hundred Years' War, however important it was in the life of this charismatic king. We owe it to Froissart that he brings to life so vividly many of its heroes, the Black Prince, his great friend Sir John Chandos, a knight of Derbyshire, the first Duke of Lancaster and Sir Walter Manny.

It is fascinating to try and ascertain the motives and ambitions of the twenty-five year old Edward III in embarking on the war in the first place. It is possible that Edward, in his maturity, became obsessed with the Crown of France believing that, as the nephew of Charles IV, the throne should have come to him by natural right. Believing this, he had a moral duty to his French subjects. A far more interesting theory and just as plausible is that Edward's reactions to the provocative moves of Philip VI were the psychological reactions of a boy, too long kept in subjection by his mother and her lover, and owed something to the political failure of his father. To embark on war was the only way to rid himself of his awful sense of humiliation. Probably his motives were mixed. There is every indication that Edward's claim to the French throne was serious, so that the argument that his real aim was to acquire an enlarged and sovereign Aquitaine is far from convincing. In any case, Edward was brave and chivalrous by nature and probably enjoyed war.

Froissart depicts The Hundred Years' War as essentially an aristocratic conflict, dominated by its ideals of chivalry, but he is aware or its wastefulness and cruelty. He also mentions, how much the King owed to the skill of the English archers. He shows considerable acumen, too, when he writes: "The English will never love or honour their King unless he be victorious and a lover of arms and war against their neighbours and especially against such as are greater and richer than themselves... They take delight and solace in battles and slaughter. Covetous and envious as they are, above measure of other men's wealth." In stressing the profit motive, Froissart is hardly fair to the combatants, though the war did provide the aristocracy with an increasing standard of living. The spoils of war, such as ransoms, charges for capitulation, bribes received for leaving places untouched, and the looting sometimes indulged in, were immensely profitable.

Yet the mass of people almost certainly felt apprehensive at the start of the war, nervous lest the possible annexation of France would result in an England becoming a mere dependency of a richer and more important dominion on the mainland.[2] So prevalent was this sentiment that Edward was obliged to give a public assurance that his assumption of the title of King of France in no manner prejudiced the rights of his English subjects.

In the opening stages of the war, it was essential to obtain the consent of Parliament, for during Edward III's early reign the Commons established a controlling voice in the raising of taxes. Certainly his own father's ruin and the difficulties of his grandfather had taught Edward the necessity for consulting Parliament. Although the Commons were to criticize the King for his extravagance, he on the whole avoided conflict with them. To raise money for his wars Edward was obliged to resort to all kinds of expedients. England's wealth largely depended on wool, and in Nottingham in 1336, he succeeded in obtaining a loan on every sack produced, estimating that this would bring him £70,000 per annum. He also negotiated an agreement with some rich English merchants, who agreed to buy, sell and export sacks of wool for him, at the same time receiving a monopoly for exporting it. The wool merchants at Dordrecht were naturally displeased when Edward requisitioned their stock, although compensated by bonds exempting them from the *maletote* or export duty.[3] This scheme, however, proved most costly and did not succeed in its object. Edward also resorted to massive borrowing, raising enormous loans from Lombard bankers, the Bardi, the Frescobaldi and the Peruzzi. He depended also on the newly established houses of Pole and Conduit and merchants in the Netherlands and from English wool merchants, offering as security either English wool or the duties on Guyennois wine.

At first Edward enjoyed considerable diplomatic success, taking advantage of his marriage with Philippa to forge alliances with the rulers of four small states in the borderland between Germany and France's northern frontiers. These were with the Dukes of Brabant, Hainault, Gelderland and Juliers. A far more important ally was the Holy (though excommunicated) Roman Emperor Ludwig IV, his Queen's brother-in-law.

To win his co-operation Edward was forced to offer him an enormous bribe, but his magnificent visit to Coblenz did result in Ludwig promising to help the King of England against Philip for seven years. He created Edward, Vicar-General (or Deputy) of the Empire,[4] but the position was really one of prestige. It was at Antwerp that Edward and Philippa kept their Court during the winter 1338-1339, and it was here that Philippa's third son Lionel was born, November 29th 1338.

England was in dire peril during 1338-1340, for French privateers commanded by Nicolas Béhuchet, a former tax collector, raided and burnt Portsmouth. A few months later another admiral, Hue Quiéret, captured five English ships off Walcheren, including *The Christopher*, England's pride, a ship specially built for King Edward. All the south coast was subjected to these fierce French raids, Southampton, Dover, Folkestone and the Isle of Wight. Froissart relates "they came on a Sonday in the fore noone, to the havyn of Hampton (Southampton), whyle the people were at masse, and the Normayns, Pycardes and Spanyerdes entred into the Towne, and robbed and pilled the Towne, an slewe dyvers and defowled maydens, and enforced wyves, and charged their vessels with the pyllage and so entred agayne into their shippes."[5] On the high seas ships taking vital supplies of wool to Flanders were attacked by the French. In retaliation, the English raided Le Treport in the spring (1339), burning thirty French vessels at anchor in the harbour of Boulogne.

After the King's first campaign in 1337, an army commanded by William de Bohun, Earl of Northampton, opposed the Count of Flanders, but it was extremely costly. Edward's debts became even more desperate. Not only had he already been obliged to pawn the great Crown of England, but during 1339 he was forced to pawn likewise the crown made for his coronation as King of France.

Edward's ruthless addiction to total war anticipated the twentieth century. The great *chevauchées*, features of fourteenth century warfare, devastated the countryside, causing immense suffering, burning defenceless villages and forcing the French peasants to flee their houses. The purpose of the *chevauchées* was to exhaust the enemy. For the non-combatant, the war was a nightmare. The open country was defenceless against these ruthless raids. For the refugee the only means to find possible safety was to conceal himself in a neighbouring fortress or walled town.

Edward's adversary, King Philip VI was cool and calculating, giving vent occasionally to terrible rages. Froissart mentions that the King of France was much influenced by the predictions of his cousin King Robert of Sicily, who enjoyed a considerable reputation as an astrologer. He had warned Philip and his Council that he must never engage in personal combat with the King of England.[6]

Edward was an active participant in two great naval battles, the Battle of Sluys and ten years later Les Espagnols sur Mer, fought off Winchelsea in Sussex. In the second conflict his ship was actually sunk under him. His subjects, delighting in their brave sovereign, gave him the proud title of 'King of the Sea'.[7]

In early June 1340, Edward was at Ipswich and 40 ships were in the Orwell ready to convey him and his retinue to Flanders. He then heard that King Philip had collected an enormous fleet at Sluys off the Flemish coast. Fearing for Edward's safety, John Stratford, the Chancellor and Archbishop of Canterbury, attempted to dissuade the King from embarking, warning him of the terrible danger he was incurring. When Edward's Admiral, Sir Robert Morley supported Stratford, the King was very angry, exclaiming: "Ye and the Archbishop have agreed to tell the same story to prevent my passage. Though ye be unwilling I will go, and ye who are afraid, where there is nothing to fear, may remain at home."[8] At first Stratford resigned the great seal to the King, but Edward later returned it to him, commanding that more ships should be assembled from northern and southern ports and from London. By the third week in June a fleet of about two hundred vessels were in the Orwell ready to sail.

The King embarked in his own favourite cog *The Thomas* commanded by Richard Fylle, the former commander of *The Christopher*, the finest ship in the English navy. These cogs were the first-class vessels of the fourteenth century, sometimes described as *escomers* or *skimmers*, warlike ships scouring the sea, playing 'the pirate'. *The Thomas* was a powerful ship of about two hundred and fifty tons. Edward was attended by many of his prominent noblemen, the Earls of Derby (Lancaster), Arundel, Northampton, Huntingdon, and the Bishops of Lincoln and Coventry. Sailing about one o'clock on June 22nd, Edward reached Blankenberg, ten miles westward of the mouth of the Sluys, where the French fleet lay in the harbour.

Various accounts of the battle are given in all the Chronicles, including Baker, Le Bel, Avesbury, Froissart and Murimuth, and there is one account in Edward's own despatch. Froissart relates that a great number of countesses, ladies, wives of knights and other damosels travelled on transit ships. They were going to the Queen's Court at Gaunt (Ghent). The King arranged that they should be well protected with 300 men-at-arms and 500 archers. It availed them nothing, for their ship was sunk, probably by cannon, and the ladies were mostly drowned. Fire-arms were certainly used in the battle of Sluys.

The French ships were fastened to each other by iron chains and cables. Four ships captured from the English, *The Christopher*, full of Genoese archers, with three other cogs, *The Edward*, *The Katherine* and *The Rose*, were in the van. Trumpets sounded in the morning air.

At eleven o'clock, Edward commanded his fleet to make sail on the starboard tack, his purpose being to gain the wind and to prevent the sun from shining in their faces. This action was misunderstood by the enemy, who said jubilantly that the English were running away. Meanwhile Sir Robert Morley, the English Admiral, bore down upon *The Christopher*, intending to recapture her.

Froissart, who relied on a first hand account of a participant in the battle, relates "then began a sore batell on both partes; archers and crosbowes began to shote, and men of armes aproched, and fought hande to hande; and the better to come togyder, they had great hokes and grapers of yron to cast out of one shyppe into another, and so tyed them fast togyder". He describes the confusion, the cries, and the massive slaughter as the English recaptured *The Christopher*. She was immediately manned with English archers, so that she could attack the Genoese galleys. Of Edward III, Froissart wrote: "The King of England was a noble knight of his owne hande, he was in the flouer of his yougth"[9] (actually he was twenty-eight). Both English and French displayed their customary bravery, and among the most gallant the Earls of Derby, Northampton, Sir Walter Manny and Sir John Chandos.

In a famous passage Froissart writes: "This batayle was right ferse and terryble: for the batayls on the see ar more dangerous and fierser than the batayls by lande; for on the see ther is no reculyng nor fleying."[10]

It was probably the superiority of the archers that gave the victory to the English in this fierce battle, which lasted from ten to twelve hours. In the confusion, many of the enemy jumped into the sea. Two French admirals were captured, the

badly wounded Hue de Quiéret, who was immediately beheaded, and Nicolas Béhuchet, whose body was hung on the
yard-arm of *The Thomas* (Edward's flagship), greatly alarming
the French sailors.

The Battle of Sluys was a complete victory over a brave
enemy, gaining enormous prestige for King Edward, but it did
not give England command of the seas. However, it increased
England's renown and was important in establishing her naval
supremacy. One beneficial result was psychological, the confidence acquired in defeating the French, who greatly outnumbered them both in ships and men.

Edward wrote his own account to his eldest son, the
Prince of Wales, then aged ten, from his flagship *The Thomas*,
relating how *The Christopher* and the other ships had been re-
captured, and telling the boy of the enormous French losses.
The prince received his father's letter at Waltham Abbey about
June 30th or July 1st.

Since none of Philip VI's courtiers dared to tell him of the
disastrous outcome of the naval battle, his court fool was deleg-
ated to do so.

After the battle, Edward made a pilgrimage of thanks-
giving to the Shrine of Our Lady of Ardernbourge, later commemorating "Sluys on a new gold coin, the noble of six
shillings and eightpence",[11] the first gold coinage to be struck
since 1257. Then on horseback he made his way to Ghent to be
received with joy by his Queen, who was about to give birth to
her fourth son John, later to be famous in history as John of
Gaunt.

Edward returned to England in an angry mood, accusing
his Chancellor, John Stratford, his brother, Robert Bishop of
Chichester and the government at home of keeping him short
of money. He even wrote to the Pope that John Stratford, the
Archbishop of Canterbury, had adulterous designs on Queen
Philippa, an absurd accusation. He decided to return home
without notice, but his mood was not improved by the hazards
of the journey.

The *Brut Chronicle* contains a curious passage concerning
Edward's frightful experiences. No sooner had he embarked on

his ship, during November, than he was assailed by fearful storms of lightning and thunder. In this superstitious age it was convenient to blame French sorcerers and necromancers for the weather. The *Brut Chronicle* relates that the King's heart was full of sorrow and anguish. Upon his knees he reproached St. Mary: "Oh blessed Saint Mary, what is the cause that when I go over into France all things that are joyful, to my liking and gladsome befall me, yet when I return to England all things unprofitable and harmful befall me. But, dear lady, now mercy."

Edward landed on the night of St. Andrew's Day just before cockcrow at the Tower Watergate.[12] Finding the governor absent, he immediately ordered his arrest. He then ordered the apprehension of the financiers William de la Pole and John Pulteney, accusing them of failing to sell the wool he requisitioned at a sufficiently high price. Others, including the Chief Justices of the King's Bench and Common Pleas, he dismissed from office. Losing no time in charging Archbishop Stratford with treason and conversion of public moneys, he commanded him to answer these accusations at the Exchequer. Edward wrote the prelate that he had counselled him to cross the sea without providing him with money and horses and then had withheld supplies in order to effect his ruin. Stratford wisely sought refuge with the monks of Christ Church, Canterbury.

He was, however, a man of courage, knowing that he had considerable support in Parliament and was well able to defend himself by sustained argument. Not only had he formerly opposed Edward II, but he had defied the dictator Mortimer.

On January 1st 1342, he wrote Edward III, "Very gentle King, you have had victory of your enemies of Scotland and France and at this day are held the most noble prince of Christendom." He now warned the King that he was in danger of making the same mistakes as his father. "May it please you to know that the most sovereign thing which holds kings and princes together in due and fitting estate is good counsel and let it not displease you to remember it in your time, for by the evil counsel which Our Lord your father had, he caused to be taken, against the law of the land and the great charter, the

51

peers and other people of the land and put them to shameful death, and of others he caused their goods to be seized...and what happened to him for that cause, Sire, you know well."

Stratford was absolutely justified in adhering to his rights in his quarrel with Edward III. When he tried to enter the Painted Chamber in Westminster, the Chamberlain denied him entrance, but he forced his way in.

To oppose a medieval king was always fraught with peril, but Stratford, by his persistence, established two great principles. If Edward needed the support of his people, he must submit to the judgement of Parliament. Secondly, that peers of the realm should only be tried before their own order in full parliament. The king was forced to submit and later restored Stratford to favour. He was to continue to play a distinguished part in political affairs, acting as head of the Council while Edward was overseas during the Crécy campaign. Again in the delicate negotiations with the Papacy regarding Papal privileges in England during 1344 and 1345, Edward followed Stratford's advice.

There is a curious letter from Edward III in which he complains in a decisive manner about the enormous dissatisfaction felt in England at the immense patronage bestowed by the Popes on foreigners. "But now, which is to be lamented, the ships of this very vine are degenerated into a vile vine, and the boar out of the wood doth waste it, and the wild beast of the field doth devour it. While by the imposition and provisions of the Apostolic see (which now grow more insupportable than ever) its own goods against the pious intent and appointment of the donors, are held in the hands of the unworthy and especially of foreigners and its dignities and chief benefices are conferred upon strangers who for the most part are people at the least suspected by us, and who neither reside on the said benefices, nor know the face nor understand the voice of the flock committed to them, but wholly neglecting the care of souls, like hirelings, only seek their own profit and temporal advantage..."[13] To the English clergy he writes, no doubt thankful because of his recent miraculous preservation: "We have of late been tossed and shaken as in the swelling ocean. But although the rising billows of the sea are wonderful, yet more wonderful is the Lord above, who turning the tempest into a calm, hath in so great dangers so mercifully respected us." Edward was an orthodox Roman Catholic and in his own way very religious, but he expected God and the mother of Jesus to take his side.

V 'King Edward's Evil Deed'

Edward could never resist a fight. In his chivalrous support of a gallant lady, the hard-pressed Countess of Montfort, in 1341, he shows an attractive side of his character, but there were also dark shades.

Jeanne Countess of Montfort is Jean Le Bel's female ideal, striving desperately to preserve Brittany for her small son after the imprisonment and death of her husband.[1] She was indeed an outstanding fourteenth century woman, possessing an immensely strong character and superlative courage.

It so happened that Duke John of Brittany died during the Spring 1341, leaving no children. When John Count of Montfort, his half brother, took possession of his duchy, it was disputed by Jeanne Countess of Blois, the daughter of the late Duke's younger brother Guy, who had pre-deceased him. A niece of Philip IV of France, she was married to Charles of Blois. The Valois King now summoned both contestants to Paris, but the Count of Montfort knowing that Philip intended to recognize the Countess of Blois as Duchess of Britanny, hastened secretly to England by sea.

Since John Count of Montfort was ready to recognize Edward as King of France and agreed to pay him homage for the duchy, Edward in return promised him assistance and accepted him as Duke of Brittany.[2] His action was not altogether disinterested. On their way to Bordeaux or to Portugal, it was necessary for English ships to land at Breton ports without reprisals from Breton privateers, for the route by the boisterous Bay of Biscay was very hazardous. John de Montfort eventually managed to reach Nantes where he was besieged by his rival's French army. Having been taken prisoner, he was sent to Paris.

Froissart corroborates Le Bel in maintaining that Jeanne de Montfort was one "whom no adversity could crush" with the heart of a lion. According to Jean Le Bel, she was at Rennes when she heard that her husband had been captured. She possessed a marked military and strategic sense, equipping her fortresses and wise in her choice of heads of garrisons. Holding her infant son aloft before her soldiers, she exclaimed: "Be not afraid nor amazed for my Lord whom we have lost. He was but a single man. See here my little son, who please God, will be his restorer and who will do you much service."[3] No wonder her words aroused tremendous enthusiasm among her troops, but after the fall of Rennes - one of the chief cities of Britanny - she was besieged in her castle of Hennebon throughout the following spring. At last the intrepid lady, in a state of desperation, was forced to send her loyal knight, Sir Amaurac de Clisson, to England imploring succour from King Edward and eager that her infant son might marry one of Edward's daughters.

It is curious that in this case Edward seemed to be opposing the principle he had so ardently supported, namely that a man might inherit through a woman's rights in connection with property, though she was unable to hold them.

Edward did not hesitate to send back with Sir Amaurac over 3,000 of the best archers[4] in England under the command of the Hainaulter Sir Walter de Manny, a valiant and wise knight, dearly loved by the King. Unfortunately, terrible storms overwhelmed the expedition and they battled with the elements during sixty days.

Jeanne de Montfort was in despair, aware that her nobles were insisting that she should surrender. How alive she is in Froissart or Le Bel's chronicle, ascending the watchtower of the castle of Hennebon and gazing anxiously from a window out to sea, and no doubt praying with anguish for the long awaited help. At last in Froissart's words, "She began to smyle for great joy" for low on the horizon fluttered the sails for which she craved. "I see the succour I have so long desired" she cried "I see the ships." Always kind and tactful, she came down from her castle and kissed her deliverers, Walter de Manny and his companions, two or three times. Later, during the summer (1342) Lady de Montfort's infant son was received at the English Court, joining the royal nurseries of Queen Philippa, but he did not marry one of the princesses.

We see here the strong chivalrous trait in Edward's character, in seeking to save a lady in distress, but Le Bel, his ardent admirer, describes one evil, foul deed committed by the King in 1341 or 1342 with such obvious reluctance, yet with such realism that it is difficult to believe it is not the truth. Indeed, Le Bel's value as a historian was his adherence to what he perceived to be the truth. Froissart may be far more charismatic as a chronicler, but he is less concerned with accuracy. Much of the early part of his chronicle owes a great deal to Le Bel, a man of considerable personal magnificence, always splendidly and fashionably attired and an accomplished horseman.[5]

There are at least two contemporary authorities for the alleged rape by Edward III of the Countess of Salisbury, the full story of this *villain Cas* in Le Bel, and in the *Chronique Normande du XIVe siècle*.[6] Froissart, however, expressly condemned Le Bel's story, inserting in 1345 a strong criticism of its veracity. He wrote: "You have heard me speak above of Edward's love for the Countess of Salisbury. The Chronicle of Jean Le Bel speaks of this love less properly than I must, for, please God, it would never enter my head to incriminate the King of England and the Countess of Salisbury with such vile accusation..."

Antonia Gransden discusses the whole problem in an interesting article,[7] but she alleges that Le Bel relied on a French source. This sought to discredit Edward III for propaganda purposes and is far from convincing. It is much more likely that Le Bel heard an account of the affair from somebody present in the castle when the alleged rape took place. Antonia Gransden writes that "this tale is full of improbabilities and impossibilities, and its author may have taken as a literary model Livy's story of the rape of Lucretia." She rightly stresses some serious inaccuracies in Le Bel's account, but that does not signify that it is untrue. One thing that is clear however, is that Le Bel was a scrupulous, truthful historian of integrity, and disapproved of writers falling beneath this high ideal. Is it likely that he would include a fictitious episode in his work? This aspect of his character is strongly stressed by Diana Tyson.

It is probable that Edward did rape a lady, but that she was not the Countess of Salisbury. Le Bel says that her name was Alice, but the wife of Edward's intimate friend, William Montagu, bore the name of Katherine. Katherine Grandison was certainly not the lady so ardently loved by Edward in 1341-1342. She had been married to the Earl for fourteen years, and the King would have known her well, particularly as she had served as royal governess to his children in the palace of Woodstock. She is later known to have died during the Black Death in 1349.

Nor is it conceivable that the lady in question was Alice, the aged widow of Thomas of Lancaster, whose matrimonial career and sexual adventures had gained her some notoriety. It is more likely that Le Bel could have confused the Countess Katherine with the wife of Edward Montagu, younger brother of the first Earl of Salisbury. Her name was Alice, the youngest of the three children of Thomas of Brotherton, Earl of Norfolk, a half-brother of Edward II. Not only a co-heiress, but very beautiful. Born in 1324, she had been married at the age of thirteen to Sir Edward Montagu, twenty years her senior. After her father's death in 1337, Alice Montagu was the owner of Bungay Castle and valuable estates in Suffolk. She would have been seventeen in 1341.

Despite his happy marriage to Philippa, Edward at twenty-nine was young and lustful, not accustomed to being thwarted in his passions. Froissart describes the King "stryken therewith to the hart, with a sparcle of fyne love that endured long after, he thought no lady in the worlde so worthy to be loved as she."[8] Froissart's idolized picture of Edward is romantic, but was his intention to conceal the truth?

Edward's attempt to seduce the Countess of Salisbury occurred, according to Froissart, at Warke Castle in Northumbria. Warke was then under the constant threat of attack by the Scots during December 1341. The castle of Warke-on-Tweed had been granted by the King to the Earl of Salisbury in 1329 for life (or in 1333 in fee tail). Salisbury was absent from the country from Easter 1340 until early in June 1342, held prisoner in France, but in his absence his brother, Sir Edward Montagu, a fierce hard-bitten soldier, had been appointed Governor of Warke Castle. There is no known evidence that Katherine, Countess of Salisbury was at Warke during December 1341, but a young, lovely lady, possibly Lady Alice Montagu, had been left as chatelaine of Warke Castle. One dark night, drenched to the skin and exhausted, Edward Montagu arrived at Newcastle, seeking the King's help. Excusing Montagu from attending on him, the King made for Warke Castle where he was hospitably entertained by a virtuous and strong-minded lady. It is evident from Froissart's account that though Edward was much in love with the lady, she resisted his advances. All the King's attendants noted that their master was pensive, nay sad and not merry and laughter-loving as was his wont. Frustrated, the King rode northward, passing an unhappy Christmas at Melrose Abbey. On his return journey southward, passing in the neighbourhood of Warke Castle, Edward sent the lady a message by her nephew William Montagu, son of the imprisoned Earl, "that she should rejoice since he, the King, had her husband's welfare much in mind." Froissart, if one is to believe he was aware of the real truth, paints the whole episode in a most romantic light, without the slightest criticism or condemnation of Edward's behaviour. This was possibly to spare Queen Philippa, his patron, from any embarrassment or pain.

However, Le Bel's dramatic and highly-coloured account smacks of the truth. He heads Chapter 65 with the scandalous words "How King Edward gravely sinned when he ravished (*efforcha*) the Countess of Salisbury.' The meaning of *efforcha* in this sense is raped. It is not known where the rape occurred, but almost certainly it was in 1342 and not in Warke Castle. Le Bel wrote: "And so it was that the King stayed all day and night, but never could get from the lady the answer agreeable to him, no matter how humbly he begged her."

The night came and the exasperated Edward was in his bedchamber, knowing that the lady had also retired to her bedchamber. There was deadly silence in the Castle as Edward told his valets "that nothing must interfere with what he was about to do, on pain of death." So it was that he entered the lady's chamber, then shut the doors of the wardrobe so that her damoiselles could not help her, then he took her and gagged her mouth so strongly that she could not cry out more than two or three times, and then he raped her so brutally that "never was a woman so vilely treated and he left her lying there, all battered about, bleeding from the nose and the mouth and elsewhere, which was for her great damage and great pity." The King apparently ashamed of what he had done, left for London the following day without saying a word. The account is all the more convincing because of Le Bel's ardent admiration for the King. How reluctant he must have been to relate it. Earlier he had written "the noble King Edward who was full of all nobility and goodness for never have I heard tell any evil deed (*chose villaine*) of his save one...and the force of love drove him to it (*luy fit faire*)."

Yet the brutal means by which the King sought to have his way with the lady seems absolutely out of character. Why did Le Bel, known for his love of truth, embellish the details? Is it possible that the King, maddened by the lady's resistance, had drunk too deeply? He was known to be fond of good claret.

What adds credibility to Le Bel's story is the statement in *Le Chronicle Normande*, declaring that the wife of the Earl of Salisbury was raped (*par force violée*) by the King of England.

According to Le Bel's further account, the Earl of Salisbury was grief-stricken when he reached home and listened to the confession of his wife, particularly as Edward had rewarded his faithful service with such manifest ingratitude and base behaviour. Promising to give half his property to the Countess and their son, he left for London and the Court to accuse the King of raping his wife. He said: "Neither you nor anyone else in this land will ever set eyes on me again." Thereupon he left to fight the Moors in Spain and was killed at the Siege of Algeciras.

This part of Le Bel's story is mostly untrue. There is no record whatsoever of this bitter quarrel between Edward and his intimate friend the Earl of Salisbury. Nor is there any evidence confirming the Earl's alleged arrangements for his property, since on his death in 1344 his widow, the Countess

Katherine, had dower in his possessions and five years later William Montagu second Earl of Salisbury, had livery of the inheritance in accordance with the usual procedure. Furthermore, Le Bel's statement that the Earl of Salisbury was killed at Algeciras is doubtful, because it is known that William Montagu was killed during the Tournament of Windsor during April 1344.

Though we may accept Le Bel's account that King Edward raped some lady as substantially true, there are serious inaccuracies. Both Le Bel and Froissart are mistaken as to her identity. Nor is it conceivable that the lady concerned was Joan the 'Fair maid of Kent', secretly married, when about twelve, to Sir Thomas Holland. In 1341 and 1342 she would have been barely thirteen or fourteen. She was daughter of Edward II's half-brother, Edmund Earl of Kent, described by Froissart as the most beautiful woman of her age. She was only briefly the Countess of Salisbury, wife of William Montagu, second Earl during the late 1340s and she is reputed to be the lady who dropped her garter while dancing with Edward III at a state ball in Calais.

The consequences of Edward's lustful action were more than likely fraught with tragedy. If we accept the theory that Alice, the young and beautiful wife of Sir Edward Montagu, aged eighteen, was the lady raped by Edward III in 1342, it might fit the picture. However, Alice Montagu is a shadowy, very pathetic character in history. Le Bel says that she was battered to death by her husband almost immediately after the episode of 1342. But he is wrong as to the date. She actually lived on for another nine years until 1351. There is no doubt Edward Montagu, a brave soldier turned cattle-thief, was deeply affronted, but that would hardly justify such a brutal crime. *Cockayne's Complete Peerage* relates "that Monsiur Edward (de Montagu) William Dunche and Thomas parson of the Church of Kelleshall (Suffolk) by force of arms and feloniously did beat Alice, daughter of Thomas of Brotherton, cousin of our lord the King and wife of the said Mons. Edward at Bungay (Suffolk), that is to say on the Sunday next after the feast of Saint Butolph in the twenty-fifth year of the reign of the

King who now is (June 19th 1351) from which beating Alice languished sick unto death, and she died within the year and the day."[10] Possibly Edward Montagu was in desperate need of money, because the Bungay estates in his wife's name had been badly affected by the Plague of 1349. It is curious, however, that Edward Montagu was never prosecuted for his crime!

It is possible today to visit the ancient church of the Holy Trinity in Bungay with its shields of the Bigods, Earls and later Dukes of Norfolk. Nearby, is the ruin of Bungay Castle, strangely silent now, as though brooding with a sense of violence of that terrible scene over six centuries ago.

Galfridi Le Baker relates that Edward quarrelled with the citizens of London during 1341.[1] The Londoners were always very jealous of their liberties. When the King sent out Justiciars into every shire to enquire about the collection of various taxes, including that on the woollen commodity, the people made strong objections. "And because the citie of London would not suffer that any such officers should sit (*sederent*) as justices within their cities as inquisitours of such matters, contrary to their liberties, the King provided that these justices should hold their sessions in the Tower of London." When the Londoners stubbornly held out for their rights, Edward was highly offended (*graviter offensus*), demanding the names of those who had caused the trouble. However, the King was eventually pacified and forgave the offences committed by the Londoners. He was always wise enough to give way, if necessary, unlike his grandson Richard II, who fifty years later, was fatally to antagonize the citizens of London.

All the chroniclers tell of Edward's love of jousting. Baker relates a great jousting at Langley (so loved by his father), "for the honour of the noble men of Vasconia, which be trained up there in feates of war". Windsor, Edward's birthplace, however, always held the first place in his heart. He really loved the royal town *Windleshore*, as the Saxons called it, with its silvery Thames.

If Edward is justly to be regarded as a great king, it is surely for his imaginative zeal in founding a noble order of chivalry, inspired by the magic and the lustre of King Arthur's name. Le Bel compared him to King Arthur, so well-beloved was he in his early reign and his Court, so sumptuous.

The Order of the Garter has endured for over six hundred years, while Edward's victories on land and sea, glorious as they seemed to his contemporaries, have not. Who will ever know exactly when Edward decided that he would found a new knightly Order? Perhaps the idea slowly matured in his mind when he was returning from one of his foreign expeditions or as he ruminated in the Castle of Windsor about England's patron saint, St. George. Froissart, in his embellished account, relates "About this time (the 1340s) the King of England resolved to rebuild and beautify the gret Castle of Windsor which King Arthur had first founded in time past, and where he had erected and established that noble Round Table from where so many gallant knights had issued forth and displayed the valiant prowess of their deeds of arms over the world."[2]

Edward's dramatic instinct, one of the few qualities he inherited from his father, was deliberately used to cultivate his heroic image. And so, during January 1344, a magnificent tournament was held preceded by a splendid banquet in St. George's Hall. It was an interval of truce and Edward's guests came from every part, even from Scotland and France. Logs blazed in the vast hall, casting weird shadows on its walls as the lords and knights with their beautifully attired ladies sat down to the feast while minstrels played soft music in the gallery. Queen Philippa was there, most nobly adorned, and there, too, was her mother-in-law Isabella of France, making a rare appearance at her son's Court from Castle Rising.

It was like a resplendent scene in a theatre with Edward, richly dressed in a gown of regal velvet, with the crown on his head and sceptre in hand, walking majestically after mass, followed by Henry of Derby (representing his father, the Earl of Lancaster) and William Montagu, Earl of Salisbury, then came Philippa the radiant Queen and her son Edward, now aged fourteen, recently created Prince of Wales. His father now took a solemn oath "that he would begin a Round Table in the same manner as the Lord Arthur, formerly King of England appointed it, namely to the number of three hundred knights, a number always increasing, and he would cherish it and maintain it according to his power." It was an occasion which came to symbolize the glory of Edward's reign, but on January 30th the jousts were marred by the accidental death of the Earl of Salisbury, at the age of forty-two, from an injury sustained during the mock battles.

1344 is the date of the Round Table, but it is probable that the Order of the Garter was not founded until June 1348. The story that the first garter to be dropped was by a beautiful lady, Joan the Countess of Salisbury, with whom Edward was in love, while he was dancing with her at a magnificent ball to celebrate the capture of Calais, is accepted as the truth by historians today.[3] The King, after fastening the garter round his own knee, said the famous words "Honi soit qui mal y pense", while his courtiers sniggered.

Joan the Fair Maid of Kent as she was called, was not only beautiful but very amorous, according to Froissart. She was a cousin of the King's, the daughter of Edmund Earl of Kent (Edward II's half-brother). We first hear of Joan as a political prisoner in her home at Arundel Castle, but in her infancy she was adopted by Queen Philippa. As a little girl of nine she may have attended the historic 'feast of the heron' in 1337 in the great hall of Westminster Palace, when Edward III vowed to conquer France. She was barely twelve when she secretly married a young, valiant Lancashire squire Sir Thomas Holland. Later, since she dared not divulge her first marriage, Joan was forced to marry William Montagu, second Earl of Salisbury. Unwilling to accept his early love as the wife of another man, Holland petitioned the Pope that he should annul Joan's marriage to Salisbury and restore her to him. His Holiness agreed to do so.

Polydore Vergil, in the sixteenth century, said that the original garter belonged to a lady beloved by Edward III. Christopher Hibbert,[4] however, mentions Dr Margaret Murray's original theory and belief that in Edward's time Christianity had not yet overthrown the old religion of witches and devil-worshippers. She believed that the garter was a symbol of deep significance in that ancient religion. The Countess of Salisbury in dropping her garter was deeply confused, but not owing to the shock to her modesty. Her possession of the garter showed that she was not only a member of the old religion, but that she held the highest place in it. This ancient belief has never gained wide acceptance.

For the rebuilding of Windsor Castle, hundreds of skilled tradesmen were employed from all over the country. Among the most experienced was William Hurley[5] the King's carpenter, who was commissioned to make an enormous Round Table. However, according to the chronicler Murimuth, it was never completed. William Ramsey, the King's mason, was commanded to build a great Circular Tower. All this work was interrupted owing to King Edward's pressing need to continue the war with France.

Edward III was certainly fortunate in his magnates, especially in his cousin, Henry of Derby, only two years older than his sovereign. Henry of Grosmont as he was known from the place of his birth, succeeded his father, poor old Henry Wryneck (so Froissart called him) as Earl of Lancaster in 1345. He was to play a major role in the first phase of the Hundred Years' War, as a brilliant soldier, a successful diplomat in shaping England's foreign policy and a nobleman who enjoyed Edward's deepest confidence and trust. There was never the slightest hint of any discord in their relations. Like his royal master, Lancaster enjoyed life to the full. He was tall and fair, fond of dancing and the ladies. Despite serving on fifteen military expeditions, in which he sometimes held the supreme command, Lancaster found time to supervise the administration of his vast estates and to take part in crusades to Algeciras and to North Africa against the Moors. Also to Prussia against the Slavs. On one occasion when King Edward owed debts of £9,450 to creditors in Malines and Louvain, Henry of Grosmont possessing an admirable sense of loyalty, offered himself as one of the sureties for the debt and went to prison overseas.

He was typical of the aristocracy of the mid-fourteenth century in sharing with the King a passionate delight in tournaments and joustings. To mark his friendship, Edward III gave him, at a tournament at Eltham, a hood of white cloth embroidered with men dancing in blue habits buttoned in front with pearls. Later in 1351 (March 6th), having been rewarded with the high honour of a dukedom, the Duke of Lancaster headed a mission of 50 knights to Calais during December, where he was received by the Marshal of France, Jean de Clermont, who accompanied him to Paris.

Yet at heart Henry of Grosmont was a strangely humble man, humorous but lacking pomposity. He founded a great collegiate church at Leicester, and because of his friendship with the much venerated and sporting Abbot Clown, he granted the great Abbey of St. Mary de Pratis at Leicester, various cherished privileges.[6] A deeply religious man, he was author of a treatise *Le Livre de Seyntz Medicines* and a book of devotions called *Mercy Gramercy*. His home in London was the great palace of the Savoy, where he fathered a family, including his enchanting daughter Blanche. She married King Edward's fourth son John of Gaunt, while another daughter became the wife of Lord Henry Percy of Alnwick Castle. Ironically it was Lancaster's grandson, Henry Bolingbroke who was to usurp the throne of Edward III's grandson Richard II at the end of the fourteenth century.

Edward's grand projects for building at Windsor and elsewhere were interrupted in 1345 by the necessity of renewing the war with France. About this time he acquired an invaluable ally in Godfrey of Harcourt, a French nobleman who had quarrelled with Philip VI. Thirsting for revenge, after having been banished from his ancestral estate of St. Sauveur Le Vicomte, Godfrey had no hesitation in deserting to the English. The instinct of nationalism was not fully developed in that age.[7] To compensate Philip for Godfrey's desertion, John of Hainault, attracted by the higher pay offered by the King of France, agreed to serve him, and we find him fighting with the French at Crécy against his former friends and allies. Another unreliable friend was the tricky Duke of Brabant.

Both Edward and Philip might feign to pursue negotiations with the Pope to renew the truce, but they were working hard at the same time to increase their armed forces. Although the French envisaged that the English intended to invade Flanders, Edward eventually decided on the advice of Godfrey of Harcourt to assail Normandy. This nobleman knew intimately the rich countryside with its farmlands. He therefore told

Edward that the people of Normandy were not accustomed to war.[8] As the great towns were to some extent unwalled, his soldiers would find such an invasion highly profitable and so it proved.

The Crécy campaign is memorable for many things, not least that Edward the Prince of Wales, now aged sixteen, the usual age for a prince in the medieval age to be given a military command, experienced active fighting in 1346.

VII Crécy

It is meet to discuss the famous English longbow, so deadly a weapon in the hands of the English archers at Crécy. It was of Welsh rather than English origin, having been used in the twelfth century during campaigns in Gwent. Later it became the characteristic weapon of the English mounted archers fighting in Edward's campaigns in Scotland during 1334/1335. To discharge their arrows it was necessary for them to dismount quickly. An experienced longbowman could shoot ten or twelve arrows a minute, and their rapid hail against an advancing army, both demoralizing the enemy and maddening the horses, was particularly effective. These enormous six-foot bows of yew, maple or oak had several advantages, for their range was about 275 yards and they were capable of penetrating chain armour. They were much less effective above 165 yards. However, the longbow had its limitations, being essentially a defensive weapon, and most effectively used against advancing enemy cavalry, it was no use whatsoever if the enemy failed to advance or if the site of battle was ill-chosen. The longbow was peculiar to the English armies, while the French armies contained crossbowmen always fighting on foot with a few mounted archers. These were composed of separate companies under constables. During the fourteenth century the most skilled crossbowmen were Genoese mercenaries, to be found in the French army at Crécy, but hardly employed at all in the English army.

Then there were the men-at-arms, including knight bannerets (paid 4s a day), knights bachelors (2s a day) and esquires (1s a day). Men-at-arms were always mounted, but they sometimes dismounted if it seemed advantageous to do so. They carried a lance of ten to twelve feet in length made of wood, but terminating in a metal spearhead or *glaive*, also a long sword and a short dagger known as a *misericord* or mercy, for it could be used to dispatch the mortally wounded. Among his weapons was a truncheon or axe. The Flemish foot-soldiers often carried a pike of about six feet in length, with a heavy spearhead, a deadly weapon for their unfortunate victims.

To protect himself, the man-at-arms usually wore a *haulberk*, a coat of mail, made by riveting or soldering together small rings of iron or steel, or a *colte ganboisée*, a quilted tunic comprising various materials or made of leather, sometimes stuffed with cotton or silk flock. They nearly always wore leather surcoats or *jupons*. The light cavalry or *hobelars* (paid 1s a day) wore light armour such as metal hats, steel gauntlets and so-called 'jacks', short quilted coats with iron studs. To protect the head, *bascinets* were much used by 1346, having gradually superseded the great cylindrical helms formerly worn. The *bascinets* protecting the heads of the French King's nobles had snout-like visors giving breathing holes.[1] One hears so much of the sufferings endured by the war-horses of the rival armies in medieval warfare that it is at least comforting to know that they were well protected with armour known as *bards*. The most valuable war-horse was worth well over £100.

Cannon was almost certainly used at Crécy, though the English chroniclers are strangely silent about it, but more of this anon.

During the entire winter of 1345 and spring of 1346, Edward was making massive preparations for the invasion of Northern France.[2] His army, concentrated at Portsmouth and Southampton, consisted of 15,000 men, memorable because it was over twice as large as any expeditionary force previously crossing the Channel. About 2,000 were specially selected troops, and 2,000 were men-at-arms. At first Edward was faced with frustrating delays, for during May and June strong contrary winds blowing from the south-west prevented the fleet from sailing. Then on July 11th the King ordered the whole fleet to weigh anchor, intending to land on the Cotentin peninsula, at Saint Vaast-de-la-Hougue, 18 miles east of Cherbourg. In his decision, Edward was undoubtedly influenced by

Godfrey of Harcourt's advice that he should land in Normandy.

However, no sooner did the King set forth on land than he had a nasty fall, whereupon his superstitious knights, according to Froissart, seeing his nose bleed, begged Edward to re-embark, thinking it an evil omen. However, the King bravely made light of the misadventure, declaring, "Why, this is a good token for me, for the land desyreth to have me"[3] (to embrace me). His first act was to knight the Prince of Wales and several others. In Barfleur, a flourishing town, the English were astonished at the amounts of silver and gold and rich jewels they could lay their hands on.

War might have been immensely profitable for many in Edward's army, indulging as they did in wholesale plunder and looting, and devastating the rich Norman countryside with its farms, orchards and mills, but for the French peasants it was heart-rending to see their rude homes destroyed and to be made refugees. War is always cruel, but the accounts of contemporary chronicles show the magnitude of the sufferings of the innocent civilian population, the men helpless while their women were violated and they themselves, tortured to reveal the existence of any treasures they possessed. Edward's *chevauchées* were designed to inspire terror, a kind of medieval total war.

How far did Edward condone the excesses of his soldiers? It is hard to say. For a fourteenth century king, he was hard-hearted rather than cruel. However, although he approved of a limited amount of pillaging and burning, indiscriminate pillaging, so wantonly pursued, was against his orders. The contemporary eyewitness, Michael Northbough wrote home that "much of the town (Carentan) was burnt, for all the King could do". He may have been powerless to prevent it. The wild Welsh and Irish mercenaries were not the only offenders, for the troops whose homes were on the south coast, in Portsmouth or Southampton, longed for revenge for the burning of their towns by French sailors.

Le Baker exactly describes the route of Edward's march in the Crécy campaign from La Hougue to Calais, but there is a lack of dates.[4] At Saint Lo, "a rych towne of drapery and many rych burgesses" where Edward arrived on Saturday July 22nd, his men indulged in wanton robbery, especially of precious cloth.

Four days later, Edward's army reached the historic old town of Caen. There was some tough fighting at the bridge of St. Pierre, but the garrison after some gallant resistance was forced to surrender. Then the English in pursuit, according to Froissart, "slewe many, for they toke non to mercy". Maddened by the indiscriminate plunder, the rapes and the slaughter in the streets, the inhabitants mounted to the roofs of their houses hurling stones, wooden beams and iron bars on the heads of the English soldiers, killing more than five hundred. This "sorely displeased the King", who in a fit of passion ordered that the whole population should be put to the sword and the town burnt. However, Godfrey of Harcourt managed to persuade Edward to mitigate his anger. He told him that many people would defend their homes, making it certain that there would be a serious loss of lives among his soldiers. Edward said to Sir Godfrey: "You are our marshall, ordayne every thyng as ye woll. Nevertheless there were done in the towne many yvell dedes, murdrers and roberyes."

The ransoming of wealthy prisoners was an extremely profitable business for Edward and his soldiers, since many burgesses and knights were transported in ships back to England together with jewels and vessels of gold. Among the important prisoners captured by Sir Thomas Holland, Princess Joan's husband, were the Constable of France and the Earl of Tankervyll. King Philip is reputed to have paid for them twenty thousand nobles. Holland was at least chivalrous enough to prevent many ladies and damosels from being raped by the soldiers.

The King was a born propagandist. Among the valuables captured at Caen was Philip VI's *ordonnance* for the invasion of England. Edward had copies made and ordered them to be read in every parish church in England, including St. Paul's. The object was to rouse the people, said the Archbishop of Canterbury from the pulpit. Edward remained five days in Caen not only for the purpose of dispatching the wounded prisoners and spoils of war, but his troops needed rest, having marched 82 miles in nine days.

Then on July 31st the army resumed its march towards Paris, finally stopping at Poissy having burnt Saint-Germain en Laye, St-Cloud and Bourg La Reine, according to Froissart. The people of Paris feared when their King departed for St. Denys he was leaving them to the mercy of the English, but Philip rightly calculated that Edward had no intention of approaching nearer to Paris. For his part Edward, aware that he had no siege-train and that his troops were greatly outnumbered by Philip's army at Saint-Denys, had no such intention either.

At Beauvoisin the King lodged for a night at "a fayre abbey" after giving his troops a stern order that on pain of death they were not to set on fire or burn any church or abbey. When he realized that he had been disobeyed, he had twenty men, involved in the burning, hanged.[5]

The English army's most difficult operation was the crossing of the river Somme because the bridges had been broken down by the French. Fortunately for King Edward at this critical juncture, a local peasant informed him that there was a sandy-bottomed ford just below Abbeville by which it was possible to cross. However, there ensued a sharp, bitter struggle. As the English troops strove to reach the opposite banks, they were greeted by showers of arrows from enemy troops, including mercenary Genoese crossbowmen, but they replied with a hail of their own arrows. Safely across the Somme, the English marched nine miles to the border of a forest, north-east of Blanchetaque. This forest bordered the little river Maye and beyond it lay the village of Crécy-en-Ponthieu.

In deciding to make his defensive position on a ridge 2,000 yards long called *La Vallée des Clercs* north-east of Crécy, Edward acted wisely. You can still see the site of the *moulin* where Edward directed the battle, strangely exciting after more than six hundred years. The *Vallée des Clercs* is named so because Edward, immediately after the battle, ordered his clerks to count the dead persons, characteristically making them indicate the social status of the nobility. On the highest point of the ridge commanding a fine view of the countryside stood a windmill and this the King chose as his own post of command.[6] Both his flank and his front were well protected by the river Maye and the dense wood of Crécy. It was Saturday August 26th 1346.

The English army numbered between 12,000 and 13,000 troops, but it was heavily outnumbered by the French, who were probably about 40,000 in strength. The young Prince of Wales[7] lead the vanguard consisting of 4,000 men, being able to count on experienced warriors such as Sir John Chandos and Godfrey of Harcourt. William de Bohun, Earl of Northampton and the Earl of Arundel, both valiant soldiers and friends of Edward, were in command of the rearguard consisting of 2,000 archers and 800 dismounted men-at-arms, while the King himself commanded the third division of 2,000 archers and 700 men-at-arms.

One reason why Edward was so successful in war for many years was his wise choice of commanders. Another was his personal magnetism, his ability to inspire his men to give of their best. Mounted on his white palfrey, with a white rod in his hand, he rode slowly along the line of his troops before the battle, speaking words of cheer and encouragement. As Froissart relates: "He rode fro renke to renke, dyspyringe every man to take hede that day to his right and honour. He spake it so swetely and mery chere, that all suche as were dyscomfited toke courage in the seyng and heryng of him."[8] All great commanders such as the Duke of Marlborough took care of their men. Understanding their needs, the King told them to take their ease on the earth, their bows by their side and to eat and drink in moderation, so as to be fresher for the enemy. Already, we are told, he had risen very early that morning to hear mass with his son the Prince of Wales.

The regular contingents of the French army at Crécy consisted of King Philip's retinue of household troops and Genoese mercenaries under the command of Ottone Dorian.[9] The foreign notabilities had their own contingents, the valiant, old blind John, King of Bohemia, John Count of Hainault, who had deserted his brother-in-law Edward III, and James I, King of Majorca. Lastly the provincial levies. It is strange how faulty Philip's intelligence service was, for he was absolutely in the dark as to the position of the English troops. When the King of France discovered his mistake, it was already afternoon as the army started on its descent to the valley of the Maye. Then the French army changed the direction of its march, leading to demoralization in its ranks, and lack of discipline.

On being informed of the enemy advance, Edward ordered the trumpets to sound. Then the knights hastily donned their armour and the bowmen stirred themselves, brimming over with confidence.

The French were in great disorder. While those in front tried to halt, the men-at-arms behind kept on coming forward. The Genoese crossbowmen were tired, saying to their constables that they had need of rest, but King Philip, realizing that his troops were in disarray, cried: "Make the Genowayes go on before, and begynne the battle in the name of God and St. Denis."[10]

It was already evening and the sun was about to set when a terrible thunder storm broke over the battlefield, preceded by a multitude of enormous crows, fearful of the tempest. The knights declared that it presaged that the battle would be hard fought. Then the storm ceased, and the sun came out straight into the eyes of the French soldiers. The crossbowmen were within one hundred and fifty yards of the English when a sharp word of command rang out, and the English bowmen let fly their arrows so thickly that it seemed like snow. What added to the terror of the Genoese were iron balls of fire also descending on them and stampeding the horses. Villani, an Italian contemporary authority, relates that cannon was undoubtedly used at Crécy. He wrote: "The English guns cast iron balls by means of fire. They made a noise like thunder and caused much loss in men and horses...the whole plain was covered by men struck down by the arrows and cannon balls." It is most probable that Villani received accounts of the battle from the Genoese soldiers, later refugees in

Italy. They might have exaggerated what had happened, though there is no reason to doubt the essence of their stories.

Geoffrey Le Baker, the English chronicler, a *clericus* living in Oxfordshire, describes the actual battle in fifty lines in Latin, but makes no mention of cannon, nor does Froissart, except in his later editions. "The English," he relates, "had with them two of the *bombards* and they made two or three discharges on the Genoese who fell into a state of disorder when they heard their roar."

The arrogant Count of Alençon, Philip VI's brother, was so incensed by what he considered the treachery on the part of the foreign mercenaries, that he shouted to the men-at-arms behind him to ride down the traitors. So there was hopeless confusion as the men-at-arms on horseback trampled the wretched Genoese underfoot. Meanwhile the English archers with beautiful precision and deadly aim, let loose their arrows.

All the chronicles mention the bravery of the blind King John of Bohemia, fighting for France together with his son Charles. Early in the battle he said to his attendant knights that he wanted to be lead so far forward "that I may strike one stroke with my swerde". So they tied all the reins of their bridles together, and riding through the archers, charged the English men-at-arms. Next day almost all their bodies still tied together were found. On hearing what had happened, the Prince of Wales so admired the King's courage that he adopted John of Bohemia's crest and motto, the three feathers with the legend Ich dien - I serve.[11]

In the course of the fighting, the division commanded by the Prince of Wales was so hard pressed that he himself was knocked off his feet. Realizing his master's perilous state, his standard-bearer Richard de Beaumont,[12] most courageously covering the boy with the banner of Wales, rescued him. Naturally the Prince's companions, the Earls of Warwick, Oxford and Sir Reginald Cobham, were extremely anxious about the Prince of Wales's safety, so they dispatched a knight, Thomas of Norwich, to King Edward asking for succour. He found Edward directing operations on the top of the little windmill.

There is no need to doubt Froissart's picturesque account. "Is my son dead or hurt?" asked the proud and anxious father. "No Sir," quoth the knight, "but he is in sore need of your aid." The King answered - and the words would remain in the memory of the messenger all his life. "Well, return to him and to them that sent you hither and also say to them that they suffer him this day to win his spurs, for if God be pleased, I will this journey (day) be his and the honour thereof." What Froissart omits to say is that Edward did in fact send twenty knights for the Prince of Wales's succour, according to Baker,[13] but he leaves a blank for the name of the leader of the relieving force. It was probably the bishop of Durham. They found the Prince and his troops seated on the ground surrounded by a heap of French corpses, quietly awaiting the next attack.

According to Froissart, there were among the English, certain rascals "that went a fote with great knyves murdering earls, barons, knights and squiers as they lay on the ground." This highly displeased King Edward, for he would have preferred them made prisoners.

The night descended on the bloody battlefield, and the fighting continued in the light of a rising moon. All to no avail for the French against the deadly penetration of showers of arrows. Casualties among the French were enormous, about 1,500 lords and knights, including the Duke of Lorraine and Count of Alençon, and well over 10,000 in other ranks, while the English losses were comparatively light. Le Bel thought the King of France owed his defeat to taking the advice of clerics. We see him in the moment of defeat, a dejected, tragic character, surrounded by barely sixty men-at-arms, wanting to mount a last desperate charge. He had been wounded in the neck by an arrow and his horse slain. After remounting, the Count of Hainault urged Philip to leave the field. "Sir" he said, "depart hence, for there is no time to lose. Lose not yourself wilfully, if ye have loss at this time, ye shall recover it again another time." Attended by John of Hainault and by four other noblemen and a small band of faithful servants, the King galloped several miles through the darkness until he reached the royal château of La Broye. The castellan came to the gates, asking, "Who is it that calleth there this time of night?" Philip exclaimed, "Open your gate quickly, for this is the fortune of France." He tarried there only long enough for a drink, then rode on about midnight accompanied by guides to Amiens where he arrived in the early hours of the morning.

After his decisive victory at Crécy, Edward's prestige soared even higher, and the English army gained greatly in reputation. Hitherto they had been little esteemed as soldiers. One of Edward's first acts on September 1st, only five days after the battle, was to write to England to order that all available cannons should be transported to him before Calais. He now embraced the Prince of Wales, saying to him he had acquitted himself most nobly. "Fair Son, God give you good perseverance." Sunday dawned so foggy that nobody could see an inch of an acre of land in front of him. Edward arranged for the monks of the abbey of Crécy-Grange to tend the wounded, and both King and Prince of Wales were present at the funeral of the King of Bohemia, who was given special honours.

Edward, however, did not allow himself to be intoxicated by such a massive victory. His natural caution soon re-asserted itself. The arguments against marching on Paris were very strong, for the King was in immediate need of supplies. He rightly calculated that the city was well fortified, that he possessed no siege engines capable of breaching the walls and that Paris had the resources to withstand a long siege. Instead, Edward decided on the capture of Calais, an objective possessing many advantages. It would not only provide a satisfactory base for future operations, but it was the shortest sea route between the army and England, and also between the borders of his Flemish allies. However, his calculations were faulty, for he little realized what stubborn resistance he would meet there.

Edward's army arrived on the western side of Calais at the beginning of October, but he soon realized that the siege would be a long one. Furthermore, the garrison had as its commander a Burgundian knight of intrepid spirit named Jean de Vienne, who by closing the gates was determined to defy the King. He hoped to hold out until the advent of winter and to force the English to withdraw. Since the little town of Calais was surrounded by sand dunes and marshes, Edward was unable to erect siege engines. Froissart, however, relates that carpenters were ordered "to make houses and lodgynes of great tymbre, and set the houses lyke stretes and cover'd then with rede and brome, so that it was lyke a lyttell towne."[14] This town was known as Nouville. These wooden houses were intended to house his troops during the bitter winter months. A market was held on Tuesdays and Saturdays and the inhabitants were invited to bring their wares.

In the course of the winter, however, the gallant inhabitants of Calais had to endure starvation and every kind of privation. Hope was temporarily revived when in July 1347 King Philip marched with an army to relieve Calais, but he dared not attack the English in their strongly entrenched position. Then the anguished inhabitants watched in desperation while the French army retreated. With their departure the gallant Jean de Vienne was obliged to appear on the ramparts to announce that his garrison was ready to negotiate.

The story of the surrender of Calais in 1347 kindles the imagination today as it evoked brave endurance in the medieval days long since vanished. We glimpse a classic example of Edward's hard-heartedness, if not cruelty. He really hated the people of Calais for their stubborn resistance, threatening in his rage that they would all be killed or ransomed at his choice. Eventually, Edward relented so far as to allow the six chief burgesses to come into his presence dressed only in their shirts with halters round their necks. We know their names from Froissart, Eustache de Saint-Pierre, Jeanne D'Aire, Jacques and Pierre de Wissart, Jean de Fiennes and André d'Ardres.

Le Bel in his honest way makes no attempt to conceal the hardness of heart (*la duretée de coeur*) of the King. He depicts Edward in his wrath, wanting the burgesses to be beheaded despite the supplications of those bold enough to plead for their lives. Among them the renowned knight Sir Walter de Manny, pleading with the King for mercy. In their favour he mentioned that the six burgesses had come of their own free will to save the people of Calais. Edward merely told de

Manny that the citizens had killed so many of his men, they must die.

Finally Queen Philippa herself, who was pregnant, knelt before her husband in tears, interceding for their lives, as she had once pleaded for those of the careless carpenters. "Ah, gentle Sir, since I passed the sea in great peril, I have desired nothing of you; therefore now I humbly require you in honour of the son of the Virgin Mary and for the love of me that ye will take mercy of these six burgesses." The King told her that he wished with all his heart that she had another request, but he would grant her wish. A few modern historians have referred to Edward's behaviour as an elaborate charade, that he never intended the execution of these devoted men (as the *Correspondence Normande* calls them) but there is no reason to doubt the contemporary chronicles.

After the surrender, the King sent food into Calais for the relief of the starving people, but he was eager to re-people it with English colonists. He subsequently turned out many of the inhabitants, because he suspected that they did not owe him any loyalty.[15]

Edward clearly wanted to impress his enemies with his power, so that he would not hesitate to wreak his vengeance on those who opposed him. Yet he respected courage in his enemies, for he treated de Vienne generously in prison, even loading him with presents in England. To the English, Calais would remain a vital seaport for two centuries, the gateway into France.

In 1347, Edward III, at thirty-five, was at the height of his popularity, happy in the adulation of his subjects, and eulogized by Parliament for his great victories. One almost feels sorry for his adversary Philip VI's misfortunes, denied grants of money by the Estates and blamed for the defeats at Crécy and Calais.

Intending to embarrass Edward while he remained at Calais, the King of France urged David, King of the Scots to invade England. About October 1346, David with a mighty force swept down through Berwick, strongly defended by the English. "Ranging over the forest of Alnewicke they wonne a certaine manour place called Luden."[16] According to Stow, an English knight named Sir Walter Selby was captured. Kneeling before David he begged the King to spare his life and to be ransomed, but he had to stand while two of his children were strangled. Selby, almost "madde with sorrow" was beheaded. The Scots then advanced through Durham, burning the countryside to Neville's Cross, a mile or two from that city. There, an English army under William de la Zouch, Archbishop of York, the Lord Percy the Warden of the Marches, and the Lord Neville of Raby awaited them.

Froissart relates that Edward's Queen Philippa, the Regent during the King's absence overseas, was at Neville's Cross (October 1346), though this is denied by several authorities. We see her, dignified and majestic, seated on her white palfrey, reminding us of Queen Elizabeth at Tilbury, recommending her soldiers to God and St. George. There she went, in Froissart's words, "fro batayle to batayle, desyryng them to do their devoyre to defend the honoure of her lorde the Kyng of Englande, and in the name of God every man to be of good hert and courage."[17] Once again the English archers were more than a match for the warlike Scots.

Neville's Cross was a fierce battle lasting from nine till noon. Many of the Scots nobility, including the Earls of Fife, Buchan and Strathern, together with divers knights and squiers were slain. However, their great axes, sharp and deadly, claimed many victims. The King of Scotland fighting bravely was wounded in the face by an arrow and captured by a Northumberland Esquire, John Copeland. According to Joshua Barnes,[18] the Esquire, immediately after making his valuable capture of David Bruce on horseback, accompanied by eight of his friends and servants rode to the strongly defended Castle of Ogle in Northumberland, distant about twenty miles.

It is evident that Queen Philippa, not unreasonably, resented John Copeland's arbitrary action in taking away David prisoner, instead of surrendering him to the Queen. She reproved him in a letter, but Copeland replied defiantly and perhaps a little arrogantly that he would not deliver the King of the Scots to any man nor woman living, but only to his sover-

80

eign lord, the King of England. So, Copeland sailed for Calais where he knelt before King Edward, excusing himself. "Sir I requyre your Grace be not myscontent with me, though I dyde not delyver the Kynge of Scothes at the commandement of the Quene."[19]

Edward knew well how to be gracious, telling him: "John, the good service that you have done us and your known loyalty and valour are of such merit that they may countervail your trespass...and shame light on them that bear you any envy or evil will." The King now told him to return home and surrender his royal prisoner to the Queen. There is no evidence that Philippa continued to bear Copeland any resentment for his earlier behaviour. Moreover, he profited greatly, for Edward gave him a yearly rent of £500, making him an esquire of his body.

David of Scotland was led in triumph on a black charger through the streets of London to the Tower. He remained a prisoner in England for eleven years until released by the Treaty of Berwick in 1357. Later, confined at Oldham in Hampshire, the rigour of his imprisonment was gradually relaxed, for it was hoped that negotiations for his ransom would come about and that he would ally himself with England. This son of the great Robert the Bruce lacked the stature of his father, being too much addicted to pleasure, and his passion for an English mistress, Katherine Mortimer. He later became a tool of Edward III.

It was after Neville's Cross that Philippa, with a bevy of beautiful ladies and damoiselles, joined her husband in Calais. Some time during his sojourn there, it is more than probable that Edward had a mistress, no casual lady, but a mysterious woman, who had him in her clutches. True, none of the contemporary chroniclers allude to it, so the allegation must be treated with caution.

Only the writers of *The Political Poems and Songs*, including the earlier one - the so-called John of Bridlington, maintain that Edward, whilst at Calais, had a concubine. It might well be, or again we may dismiss the stories as hostile propaganda. After the subjugation of Calais, Edward's court was very gay, and the satirists hastened to denounce the lascivious behaviour of the King,[20] though perhaps excusable after stern campaigns and battles. There is a ring of truth in these allegations, bearing in mind the great warrior's weakness for women and his enjoyment of ease and luxury between battles. In this aspect of his character he bore little resemblance to his grandfather Edward I. If one credits the allegations, the influence of this mistress was responsible for checking his warlike ardour.[21]

It is fascinating to conjecture her name. In the Latin poem she is designated by the name of Diana, but it was not her real name. Nor could it be Alice Perrers, his most notorious mistress from 1364 onwards. The writer of the third chapter (not John of Bridlington) would have liked to reveal more details, but feared to draw upon himself the enmity of the lady concerned.[22]

For the most part, John of Bridlington praises Edward for his great qualities for which he deserved to triumph over his enemies. He described Edward, when young, as possessing fortitude of body and mind, sobriety, chastity, justness and activity in doing good. Nobody disputes his courage. Later his character deteriorated, particularly after the death of Philippa (1369). So did Edward I's character change for the worse after the death of his Spanish-born, first Queen, Eleanor of Castile.

As already mentioned, Edward III was on the whole well served by his ministers until his later fatal decline, but one of the writers of the *Poems and Songs* mentions some great personage who enjoyed the King's friendship and confidence, but secretly betrayed him. He calls him Traulus the Stutterer. He mentions others, false and deceitful men "who carry honey in their mouths, but seek to sting the bull (Edward) from behind".[23] In making a fresh estimate of the character of this complex Plantagenet, it behoves an honest biographer to be both wary of those who eulogize him too much and equally of those intent on his denigration.

VIII The Black Death

'The Pestilence' as it was known in the medieval age, and only called the Black Death in 1550,[1] was one of the great calamities ever to befall mankind. It devastated the western world from 1347-1351, killing twenty-five to fifty percent of Europe's population and causing vast social, political and economic change. Whether borne by infected rats or fleas, bubonic plague travelled through Egypt, Constantinople and Tunisia in North Africa, then carried by Italian merchants to Messina in Sicily during October 1347. It soon spread to southern Italy.

No great city was worse affected than Florence. Its stark horror has been graphically described by Boccaccio in his *Decameron*,[2] though his statistics of a hundred thousand dead is almost certainly an exaggeration. Another macabre description is given by a contemporary Agnolo di Tura, living in Sienna, Tuscany, one of Europe's great banking centres. Italians are lovers of children, but once stricken by the pestilence "Father abandoned child, wife, husband, one brother, another, for this illness seemed to strike through the breath and the sight...It was a cruel and horrible thing...and it is impossible for the human tongue to recount the awful truth. Indeed, one who did not see such horribleness can be called blessed. And the victims died almost immediately. They would swell beneath the armpits and in their groins, and fall over while talking. Agnolo di Tura relates that none could be found to bury the dead for money or friendship. "And I Agnolo di Tura called the Fat buried my own children with my own hands...and there were also so many dead throughout the city who were so sparsely covered with earth that the dogs dragged them forth and devoured their bodies."

There was something peculiarly foul about the plague. Orvieto in the mid-fourteenth century, a town of rich vineyards and wheatfields, claimed more than five hundred victims a day when smitten by the pestilence about the end of April 1348.

In France, particularly in Paris and Rouen, the mortality was particularly marked, for the chronicle of St. Denys estimated that 20,000 people died in Paris. There is no reason to doubt this figure, but the victims seem to have been young rather than old. Nobody was immune, royalty or commoner. Tragically enough, it was at Bordeaux that Princess Joanna, Edward II's younger daughter, died during August 1348, another victim on the way to marry the Infante Pedro, the son of Pedro the Cruel, King of Castile. Bordeaux, an important city, was the centre of the wine trade.

There exists an anguished letter of her father to the Infante:

> Death, terrible to all the kings of the earth, which takes indifferently the poor and the powerful, the youth and the alluring virgin, with the aged man, without respect to person or power, has now by the subversion of the wonted laws of mortality, removed from your hoped-for embraces, and from ours, our aforesaid daughter to whom all the gifts of nature met...whereat none can wonder that we are pierced by the shafts of sorrow. But although our bowels of pity lead us to such groans and complainings, yet we give devout thanks to God, who gave her to us, and has taken her away, but he has designed to snatch her, pure and inarticulate in the years of her innocence, from the miseries of this deceitful world and to call her to heaven.[3]

Melcombe Regis in Dorset, then a thriving town, may have been the first English port where the Black Death was introduced from Gascony or Calais. We hear of a local inhabitant catching the dreaded disease in July 1348, and the plague rapidly spreading to various parts of England, to Bristol, Southampton, Plymouth and Exeter. Galfridi Le Baker dates its appearance on August 15th in Bristol, then England's second largest town with a population of 10,000 to 12,000.[4] According to contemporary chronicles, it raged so furiously "that the Gloucestershire men would not suffer the Bristol men to have

any accesse into them, or into their countrey by any meanes".
By Michaelmas the Black Death had come to London, introduced, probably directly, from ships sailing up the Thames to
London Bridge or from the west or south via roads from Bristol
and Southampton.

Jersey and Guernsey were so badly affected by the
dreaded disease that King Edward was obliged to write to the
Governor of Jersey in an undated letter:

> By reason of the mortality among the people and fishing
> folk of these islands, which here as elsewhere has been so
> great, our rent for the fishing folk of these islands, which
> here as elsewhere has been so great, our rent for the
> fishing which has been yearly paid us, cannot be now ob-
> tained without the impoverishing and excessive oppres-
> sion of those fishermen still left.[5]

London's principal stream, the Fleet, flowing into the
Thames was so choked with garbage, human and animal waste
that water barely flowed. Various factors such as the filth, the
wretched sanitation and overcrowding were allies, conspiring
to promote plague. The lanes, deep in mud and filth of all
kinds, were made worse by the servant-wenches pouring their
chamber-pots on passers-by. There were, however, attempts to
improve matters, though they proved largely ineffectual.

For instance, King Edward wrote to the mayor to com-
plain about the filth being thrown from the houses so that "the
streets and lanes through which people had to pass were foul
with human fæces and the air of the city poisoned to the great
danger of men passing, especially in this time of infectious disease." There was little enough that the mayor could do, since
many of the cleaners had died in the plague, and others were
fully occupied in carrying twenty thousand bodies to the
burial-ground.

The Black Death provided a convenient excuse for
Edward to prorogue Parliament during January 1349. It was
then stated that the plague of deadly pestilence had suddenly
broken out and daily increased in severity so that grave fears
were entertained for the safety of those coming there at that
time. Edward was secretly relieved, for Parliament had re-

cently been obdurate, extremely reluctant to grant a subsidy for three years unless taxation was reduced.

The pestilence was no respecter of persons. Among its victims may have been John Stratford Archbishop of Canterbury, staunch upholder of parliamentary rights. He had not lacked courage in standing up to Edward III. He died during May 1348, to be succeeded by John Offord, also one of its victims before being invested. Westminster, too, shared in the suffering, for Simon of Bircheston, Abbot of Westminster Abbey (1344-1349), no great loss, since he was known for his favouritism and his mismanagement of Abbey affairs, died of the plague May 15th 1349. A quarrelsome man, he came into conflict with his own prior. Twenty-six monks perished with him and they are commemorated in the East Cloister. At St. Albans the prior, sub-prior and 46 monks died.

The population of London was, perhaps, 50,000 in 1349, but the scourge of the Black Death claimed thirty-five to forty percent victims, possibly more.

East Anglia was badly affected. Norwich, a city with a population of 10,000 to 12,000 people and a very prosperous one in the middle of the fourteenth century, suffered severely, losing about half of its beneficed clergy and 40,000 of its secular population. Bury St. Edmunds in Suffolk, another flourishing town of, perhaps, 7,000 people, lost so many of its priests that Pope Clement VI gave the Abbot permission to ordain ten monks as priests.[6]

Life became more violent after the Black Death. In Bury St. Edmunds two of the monks, John de Grafton and one named Blunderston, during the 1360s were involved in a bitter quarrel with another monk, John de Norton, stabbing him to death as he lay in the Abbey dormitory. John de Grafton and his accomplice were both imprisoned for this crime for one year, but they were never brought to trial. They received a royal pardon from Edward III on the grounds that the crime had been committed in "hot blood".

When we consider the cruelty and violence so prevalent in the late fourteenth century, mindful of the piety, the superstitions, and the simple pleasures and joys of ordinary people, how terrible must this ever present threat of plague have been, tormenting the medieval mind. Men were fascinated and obsessed by death, influenced by the preachers constantly stressing the brevity of human life and earthly glory. The theme increasingly expresses itself in medieval art after 1350.

Thus, after the Black Death, changed attitudes came about. The people regarded the scourge as divine punishment upon mankind for its sins. So the city of Rouen ordained that everything that could anger God, such as gambling, coursing and drinking, must cease.

Edward and his court escaped comparatively lightly. While the plague was still raging in London, on St. George's Day 1349, the first service of the Order of the Garter was held at Windsor. A resplendent scene when the knights in their garter-blue robes took their places in the stalls. It is curious, perhaps, that Chaucer, the greatest poet of his age, then a page at Edward and Philippa's court, only makes one oblique reference to the Black Death. While the nobility could always retire to their country mansions in isolated parts of England, the poor were far more vulnerable in their squalid hovels.

The Black Death did not cause the later Peasants' Revolt (1381), but it was certainly responsible for the rise in tension after 1350, the increase in a sense of grievance and the overwhelming bitterness and despair felt by the people, which made the Peasants' Revolt inevitable. Two other insurrections causing important economic and social tensions, arising from the great pestilence, were the so-called *Jacquerie* in 1358 in France, and the *Ciompi* in Florence, an urban-industrial rebellion. Though the soldiers of the *Jacquerie* were mainly peasants, their leader Etienne Marcel and many others, were bourgeois. The name given to the *Jacquerie* ironically refers to the leather jerkins peasants wore in battle, instead of armour, which they could not afford. The bestiality of those taking part is comparable to the savage cruelty of the revolt, twenty-three years later.

Doctors could do nothing to relieve the suffering of those smitten with the plague, but there was a marked advance in surgery after the Black Death. The barber-surgeons of the earlier fourteenth century, mostly illiterate men, were gradually replaced by surgeons who had studied practical surgical manuals. Two of the most celebrated of the later fourteenth century, were an Englishman, John Arderne, who served Edward III and Guy de Chauliac, surgeon to the King of France and the Pope.

John Arderne was born in 1307, living nearly to the end of the century. For twenty-one years he practised at Newark (1349-1370) when he came to London, to be probably admitted as a member of the fraternity of surgeons. His patron was Edward's cousin, Henry Plantagenet, Earl of Derby, later the first Duke of Lancaster. After Lancaster's death from the plague (1361), Arderne may have entered the service of his son-in-law, John of Gaunt. His most famous work is *Arte Phisiscali et de Cirurgia*[7] dated 1412. In his methods of treatment Arderne was certainly well in advance of his time, original too, in his operation for the cure of fistula, still used today, though falling into disuse for nearly five hundred years. Arderne's teachings had a marked influence on surgeons for many years after his death. However, many doctors remained ignorant amateurs.

One important, immediate repercussion from the Black Death was the sharp rise in wages, for there was a shortage of labour. However, the rise in the cost of living reduced any advantage the labourer gained thereby. The Statute of Labourers[8] (1351) was an attempt to codify the wages of labourers and artisans, mainly successful in its object. For instance, various restrictions were introduced, such as forbidding a labourer to leave his place of work in search of more lucrative employment, while the employer was restrained from offering wages larger than three years before. The Statute was very unpopular, leading to much discontent and the harbouring of grievances in the minds of the labourers.

The later 1350s marked the gradual decline of the glorious reign of Edward III, yet the naval victory of Winchelsea (1350) and the battles of Poitiers and Nájera still lay in the future. Although the Victorian Stubbs is justly critical of Edward III, he is hardly fair in his appraisal of the king:

Edward was by no means a popular king or the king of a contented people. There was a great gulf between him and the body of the nation, and his reign from this time (he is referring to the 1350s) is anything but a brilliant period of history...We find a lack of good faith, an absence of national sympathy, a selfishness that repels more than else attracts.

Perhaps it is fairer to say that Edward remained a popular king while he was fortunate in war and his victories rang in the ears of the people, but many mourned their excessive cost, the extravagance of his court and punitive taxation.

IX The Garter And Its Aftermath

Polydore Vergil, writing in the days of the early Tudors, was the first to maintain that the foundation of the Order of the Garter was in honour of the female sex. As already mentioned, it is almost certain that the garter of some lady of the court fell off as she danced with the King and that Edward had chivalrously taken it from the ground exclaiming, "Honi soit qui mal y pense." Most historians have identified the lady, perhaps too readily, as Joan Countess of Salisbury, but this is far from proven. If Joan was really the garter countess, it is curious that she is not named in the earliest version of the story. According to Polydore Vergil the owner of the garter was either the Queen or one of the ladies of the King's liking. Selden, writing in 1614, records traditions relating to Joan of Kent, Countess of Salisbury. "Her garter, that falling from her leg in a dance was taken by the King, who much affected her."

John of Bridlington, a contemporary chronicler, writing in 1370, mentions "the Queen of England", alias Diana, coming to England and captivating the King. His "Queen of England", was definitely not Philippa.

Margaret Galway in her interesting article in *The Historical Journal of the University of Birmingham*, is convinced that the lady in question was the beautiful Joan, arguing that Diana was pre-eminently the huntress of the hind and hart. A white hind on red was the cognizance of Joan of Kent, later adapted to a white hart by Richard II, her younger son. However, there were other ladies at Edward's court eager enough to be his lover.

Companions of the Order numbered twenty-six, and the honour was mainly bestowed on those with a distinguished military career during the Hundred Years' War. It did not include distinguished members of the Council or Parliament. The

Tomb of Edward II in Gloucester Cathedral.

Execution of Hugh Despenser the Younger in 1326.

Corbel head of Edward III from Tewkesbury Abbey.

Battle of Poitiers.

A meeting of the Knights of the Garter in the chapel of St. George at Windsor.

Effigy of the Black Prince.

The Black Prince pays homage to Edward III.

Gilt bronze tomb effigy of King Edward III.

first twenty-six founders included the sovereign Edward III, the Prince of Wales, Henry Plantagenet Earl of Derby (later Duke of Lancaster), Thomas Beauchamp third Earl of Warwick, William Montague (Montagu) second Earl of Salisbury, Sir James Audeley, a comrade-in-arms of the Prince of Wales, Sir Thomas Holland and Sir John Chandos. It is still possible to see Chandos's exquisite stall plate in St. George's Chapel, Windsor.

George Frederick Beltz[1] mentions the ensign and habit of the Order worn by the Sovereign Founder and the Knight Companions. They were the garter, the mantle, the surcoat and the hood. The materials of the first garters were of blue cloth or silk embroidered with gold, but they differed from today's garters' blue. They are variously described to be of blue satin, tantarin of taffeta lined with buckram and braid of like colour and embroidered with cyprus and soldat gold and with silk of various colours.

The mantle is alluded to in the ancient statutes. It was somewhat similar to the *pallium* or *toga* of the Romans, worn without sleeves, covering the whole body and reaching down to the ankles.[2] However, Edward's mantle differed from that of his companions owing to the greater length of its train of woollen cloth, the chief manufacture of England. The colour of the mantle was blue, but the lining in the early days of the foundation was of scarlet cloth, while the King's lining was ermine. Under the mantle it was customary to wear the surcoat (*supertunica*), apparently in imitation of the *tunica* worn by the Romans. While the sovereign's surcoat was lined with ermine, those of 'the companions' were lined with fur of miniver. The hood, worn hanging down the back like a pilgrim's hat, was much in use in the middle of the fourteenth century.

In those early days, the chief officers of the Order were the Prelate the Bishop of Winchester, the Register and dean of Windsor or the principal canon of St. George's College of Windsor and the gentleman-usher of the Black Rod.

There are records of a payment of £500 - a gift from the King to Queen Philippa - for the preparation of her apparel against the feast of St. George (April 23rd) to be celebrated at Windsor. Other curious payments for 47s 11d are to divers messengers and runners sent into various parts of England with letters under the privy seal and signet, directed to several lords and ladies, inviting them to the feast of St. George at Windsor. William Volaunt, King of the Heralds, at the said feast was rewarded for his good services with 66s 8d, while Walter Newman and his twenty-three fellows for the carrying of oats to Windsor about the time of St. George's feast received 13s 4d. Nor were Edward III's minstrels forgotten, for Fitz Lubbin and his twenty-three fellows for their good services received £16.

It was possible for a Knight of the most noble Order of the Garter to make a formal renunciation. For instance, Edward's son-in-law Enguerrand de Coucy, a distinguished Frenchman, on his marriage to Isabella, the King's pampered eldest daughter, was created a Knight of the Garter (1365) and in the following year, Earl of Bedford, by Edward. However, eleven years later, after the boy King Richard II had succeeded his grandfather, de Coucy, influenced by sentiments of divided allegiance to the Kings of England and France after a renewal of the war, in an honourable manner signed the instrument of surrender (August 26th 1377) giving his reasons for the renunciation. Consequently another knight, Sir Lewis Clifford, was elected in his place.

The truce of 1347 continuing to 1350, owing to England and France being denuded of a third of their population by the Black Death, was rudely interrupted that summer by a great naval battle in which King Edward took a leading part. It was off the coast of Winchelsea in Sussex that Edward gained a magnificent victory over the Spanish fleet, allies of the French.

Winchelsea, an ancient village, remains today very much as Edward's grandfather Edward I planned it. There it lies, not unaware of its glorious past, with its original gates, Strand Gate, Pipewell and New Gate. There, too, is the church inspired by Edward I and dedicated to St. Thomas à Becket, with its fine carvings of the heads of Edward I and of King Edward II and Queen Isabella. While its neighbour Rye, only two miles distant, seems to bear the influence of France, Winchelsea is today very English, with its Georgian houses.

92

All that summer Castilian and Genoese galleys had been openly waging war on English shipping in the Channel. The galley was an ideal ship for raiding purposes, for she had a shallow raiding draught, being manoeuvred by oars as well as sails. She thus could penetrate inshore and did not depend on the direction of the wind as much as other vessels. Hearing that a large Castilian fleet was making up-channel for the ports of Flanders, King Edward decided to intercept it on the return voyage. So, he put to sea accompanied by some of the most important noblemen in the kingdom and by an impressive company of men-at-arms, knights and squires. Accompanying Edward were his sons the Black Prince, now in his twenty-first year and in the first flower of his manhood, and his younger brother John, Earl of Richmond later known as John of Gaunt, then aged ten. Although too young to bear arms, Froissart relates that the Black Prince, who was very fond of him, took him in his own ship. Others taking part were Henry of Lancaster (newly created a Duke), William Bohun of Northampton, the Earls of Warwick, Arundel, Salisbury and Huntingdon and John Chandos.

Edward assembled a great fleet at Sandwich numbering 50 sail, impressive enough, but insignificant in appearance to the 44 galleons, powerful vessels commanded by Don Carlos de la Cerde.

Froissart has given an immortal picture of King Edward in August 1350, standing in the bows of his favourite ship the cog *Thomas*, wearing a black velvet jerkin and a black beaver-skin cap. Never had his knights seen their sovereign in better humour, so gay and apparently carefree, and full of zest. It so happened that Sir John Chandos was in the King's ship, and to please Edward, the knight sang a song he had recently brought back from Germany. He sang in his deep rich voice to the vast enjoyment of the King and the ship's company, with the minstrels accompanying the air. Then the sailor on the look-out espied a Spanish vessel and cried "Ship ahoy". The minstrels stopped playing. Two or three Spanish ships now hove into sight, then the whole fleet, so that the sailor cried: "There are so many, God help me, I can't count them." The King ordered wine to be served, and the English donned their battle-helmets.

Galfridi Le Baker in his chronicle gives an accurate account of what happened.[3] "Upon the feast of the decollation of St. John, about evensong time, the navies mette at Winchelsea, where the great Spanish vessels surmounting our ships and feystes, like as castles to cotages sharpeley assailed our men." He relates that the Spanish hurled stones from the quarels of the top deck of their large vessels known as busses, sorely and cruelly wounding our men. They also hurled great iron bars.

During the course of the battle both Edward, and especially the Black Prince, were in acute danger, for the commander of *The Thomas* made a misjudgement in closing with the nearest Spanish ship as she passed at too great a speed and at too sharp an angle, so that there was a mighty collision. *The Thomas*, the lighter vessel, came off worse, springing a bad leak and water pouring in. Fortunately the highly trained English men-at-arms and the archers fought superbly, though Edward did not seem at first aware of the danger of his flag-ship sinking. Much against the odds, the English succeeded in capturing the opposing Spanish vessel, the King being persuaded by his knights to abandon *The Thomas* for the captured ship. Meanwhile, the Spanish crossbowmen with deadly aim were killing many English.

A large Spanish vessel had managed to inflict such powerful damage on the Prince of Wales's ship that she stood in acute danger of sinking. Fortunately Henry of Lancaster managed to sail his ship up to the Spaniard on the other side[4] and crying "Derby to the rescue", succeeded in boarding her. The Black Prince transferred to her just in time. The enemy seamen were all thrown into the sea. Many brave feats were performed by both the contestants, but the English eventually prevailed. The contemporary chroniclers differ as to the number of Spanish ships lost or destroyed. Froissart says fourteen, Avesbury twenty-four, but Baker's number of seventeen is probably correct.

This was a proud day for the people of Winchelsea, standing on the cliffs of the little harbour and cheering lustily as the great Spanish galleys were captured. After the battle the King, the Black Prince, John of Gaunt and the Duke of Lancaster rejoined the anxious Queen Philippa during the night of August 29th at Pevensey Castle. She had spent the whole day at prayer in Battle Abbey. One can well imagine the rejoicing and the revelry as the knights feasted and drank, relating their stories of love and war. The King, too, would have thanked them in his gracious way, particularly for their brave conduct. Winchelsea was a far more dangerous battle for Edward than Sluys. It succeeded, however, in providing safe communication with the King's armies in Gascony and Brittany and to clear the Channel of Spanish ships.

One can but marvel, too, at Edward's naval supremacy when we record that the French possessed a naval base at the *Clos de Galées* at Rouen, much superior to the English royal establishment at the Tower of London and at Ratcliffe below London Bridge. The three French kings, Philip VI, John II and the astute Charles V, had all been vitally concerned in preserving a powerful navy, in purchasing barges and galleys, keeping them in good repair and establishing supply depots at Dieppe and Harfleur.[5]

On August 22nd 1350, a week before the Battle of Winchelsea, there died at Nogent-le-roi Edward's adversary Philip of Valois, King of France. Except for his disastrous strategy at Crécy, Philip was not by any criterion an ineffective king, for he left France a far larger country even if he lost Calais to the English. Perhaps he best deserves to be remembered as the grandfather of a great King of France, the future Charles V, a statesman rather than a warrior.

X Poitiers And Its Aftermath

After the Battle of Winchelsea Edward was very much preoccupied taking the measure of the new King of France, John the Good (*Le Bon*). He received this appellation not for his moral qualities, but for his reputation as a "good fellow well met". He had already reached the ripe age of thirty-one when he succeeded his father. Like Edward, he had a love of chivalry, inducing him to found the order of the *Etoile*. However, John II lacked the intelligence of his father, revealing ineptitude in negotiation, as King Edward soon discovered. Outwardly he might be impressive, a large handsome man, with a thick red beard, physically brave as he later proved at the Battle of Poitiers, but as a ruler he was the slave of his passions, possessing a fatal weakness for giving way too easily to panic.

During the 1350s Edward was fortunate in his brilliant treasurer William Edington, Bishop of Winchester, who six years later also became his Chancellor. As a young man Edington had attracted the notice of Adam Orleton, who had helped his career. Knowing that it was essential to pay for the king's campaigns, he decided to centralize all government finance under the Exchequer. Edington was so adroit in his management of the finances that the king was able to refrain from asking Parliament for too much money.

About 1354 Edward acquired a new ally, the completely unreliable and treacherous Charles II of Navarre, king of a small mountain kingdom in the Pyrenees, known in history as Charles the Bad. He was of considerable importance because he possessed several counties in Normandy. He was, through his mother, a grandson of Louis X, one of the last Capets, thus having a better claim to the French throne than Edward III. However, his parents when acknowledging Philip VI as King of France, had renounced their own claim. Charles of Navarre was a subtle intriguer, able, charming, ambitious as Lucifer and a cunning murderer. One of his daughters, Joan, married Henry IV of England as his Queen.

His particular hatred was reserved for Don Carlos de la Cerda, the nobleman, who had commanded the Spanish fleet at the Battle of Winchelsea, a great favourite of King John. Charles of Navarre burnt with injustice because the King of France had bestowed the county of Angoulême on Carlos, for it rightly belonged to the kingdom of Navarre. Then John created Don Carlos Constable of France. Fearing that he had offended Charles of Navarre too deeply, he now offered him his daughter in marriage, though foolishly refused to pay any dowry. Charles the Bad at this juncture hastened to intrigue with King Edward, playing off the Valois King against the King of England. Where a strong king would have acted decisively, John II merely vacillated, pretending for some time to be reconciled to Charles of Navarre by trying to appease him.

After abortive attempts by Pope Innocent VI to achieve a settlement between England and France, the fragile peace talks collapsed. Charles of Navarre then promised to take part in a joint expedition with the English army commanded by the Duke of Lancaster, only later to back out of the undertaking. The Pope accused Edward of conspiring with Charles of Navarre against the King of France, but Edward in order to justify the renewal of the war, accused the French of perfidy.

Once again Edward showed a superb knowledge of public relations, writing letters to the Archbishops of Canterbury and York, proclaiming the righteousness of his cause and relating his grievances. While he was successful in war, he found it easier to extract money from Parliament. Throughout the busy summer of 1355, the provisioning of his army went on apace.

Edward of Woodstock, Prince of Wales, was now twenty-five, a soldier of genius as he was soon to prove himself at the Battle of Poitiers. There he revealed desperate courage. He captured the imagination of his contemporaries and later the heart of posterity even after more than six centuries, far more than his father had. He has become a legend. In many ways a fine character, he seems to symbolize the best side of the Middle Ages. Often chivalrous to his enemies, he had a magnificent taste in art, like his son Richard, and possessed what his biographer describes as "a debonair liberality".[1] He had all the Plantagenet extravagance. His faults lay in his unforgiving nature, and in his later, political career he revealed a lack of sensitivity in dealing with his subjects in Aquitaine and a deficient judgement, making it extremely improbable that he would have been a successful king had he succeeded his father. Froissart calls him "courageous and cruel as a lion".

To his vast credit Edward III always treated his eldest son most generously, naturally extremely proud of him. It is not recorded that he ever showed envy of the Black Prince's fame or prowess in war. Nor with his own high reputation in warfare would one expect it. In character the Black Prince resembled his great-grandfather Edward I, possessing something of his austerity and single-minded sternness, yet he could be gracious enough and even humble, but he lacked his father's gentle charm.

The Prince of Wales's "*Grande Chevauchée*" of September 1355 was extremely destructive of property, but its military object was to concentrate on the enemy's weakness and to deprive him of his taxes by destroying the lands on which they were levied. Setting sail on September 9th with 1,000 knights, squires and men-at-arms and 2,000 archers, the Prince disembarked in Bordeaux.

Baker's itinerary of the Black Prince's *chevauchée*[2] across the south of France from Bordeaux to Narbonne and back is very thorough, but somewhat marred by incorrect spelling. Together with his Anglo-Gascon allies, the Black Prince devastated many places, including Plaisance (burnt on October 19th) and Carcasonne (November 3rd). What delighted the English was the rich plunder and loot, the supplies of food and wine to be seized, the rounding up of cattle and the slaughter of pigs and chickens. Amidst the growing excitement, the English reached Narbonne within about ten miles of the Mediterranean.[3]

Meanwhile King John of France had been very active, summoning a mighty army, which began to assemble at Chartres in the spring (1356). During April, vowing vengeance against his feared enemy Charles the Bad, and furiously resentful that the Dauphin had succumbed to his blandishments, John galloped to Rouen attended by a powerful entourage. Bursting into the banqueting hall where the Dauphin in his capacity as Duke of Normandy was entertaining Charles of Navarre and various Norman nobles, the King seized Navarre, crying, "Abominable traitor, you are not worthy to sit at my son's table. By the soul of my father I will neither eat nor drink as long as you live."[4] Instead of ordering his execution, however, John had Navarre taken to Paris, to be consigned to prison in the Louvre. Jean Count D'Arcourt and three Norman lords less fortunate, were immediately beheaded.

While King John was nursing his resentment against the English and determined to avenge Crécy, towards the end of the summer Edward sent a powerful army under the command of the Duke of Lancaster. He planned that it should link up with the forces of the Prince of Wales. By August 1356 the Black Prince had entered Tours, but Lancaster failed to cross the Loire to join forces with him. When John reached Poitiers, his army numbered about 20,000 soldiers or more, heavily outnumbering the English army, perhaps amounting to 6,000 men.[5]

To visit the *champ de bataille* (the battlefield) today is an exhilarating experience. La Cardinerie Farm is the centre where the English forces were stationed. Everywhere there is undulating country. In the fourteenth century there lay a village called Maupertuis, and nearby the abbey of Nouaillé and a road leading to Poitiers. There is a famous hedge on either side of the Nouaillé-Poitiers road, excellent cover to conceal English archers.

Before the battle, there were the customary attempts to intercede between the combatants. Cardinal Taileyrand de Périgord, an aristocrat both "proud and haughty" ("*baldanzoso e superbo*" according to Villani), spent the whole of one Sunday riding from one army to another. Kneeling before King John, the prelate told him as Froissart relates:

> Sir, ye have here all the floure of your realme aganynst a handfull of Englysshmen...and Sir, if ye may have them accorded to you without batayle, it shall be more profitable and honourable to have theym by that maner rather than to adventure so noble chivalry as ye have here present.

The Cardinal found the Black Prince reasonable enough, for he would have much preferred to avoid battle with the French at this stage, knowing that his men laden with plunder were exhausted.[6] In all honour, however, he could not accept King John's hard terms, the unconditional surrender of himself and one hundred knights. Once again a French king made the fatal mistake of under-estimating the Black Prince. Fighting against desperate odds, he was at his best and in Chandos he had a soldier of genius. When we read the contemporary accounts of this hard fought battle, Monday September 19th, we can readily understand that victory might easily have gone to the French.

Various factors militated in favour of the English, the military genius of the Black Prince and his chief of staff Sir John Chandos, the well chosen position for defence, the clever choice of ground selected for the archers behind a hedge where they had a clear vision of lower ground in front, and the superior, united generalship of the English army.

Baker gives one of the best and most detailed accounts. He is writing two years after the battle, relying to some extent on the revelations of those taking part. For instance, the Black Prince's inspiring speech to the archers before the battle made such a strong impression that the gist of it remained in their minds:

> Your manhood hath bin alwaies known to me, in great dangers, which showeth that you are not degenerate from true sonnes of English men, but to be descended from the blood of them which heretofore were under my father's dukedome, and his predecessors Kings of Eng-

land unto whom no labor was paineful, no place invincible, no ground unpassable, no hill (were it never so high) inaccessible, no tower unscaleable, no army impenetrable...

The Prince would never accept defeat, but he told his men:

If envious fortune (which God forbid) should let us at this present, to runne the race of all flesh and that we ende both life and labour together, be you sure that your names shall not want eternall fame and heavenly joy, and we also with these gentlemen our companions will drinke of the same cuppe that you shall do.[7]

The soldiers knew that their prince would share all their dangers, and would follow him to the death.

In his tactics King John of France may have been too much influenced by a Scot, Sir William Douglas, who persuaded him that the men-at-arms, in three divisions, should march on foot in their heavy armour. In the front line was Charles Duke of Normandy, the Dauphin, together with his younger brothers Louis, Duc d'Anjou and Jean, future Duc de Berri, destined to be a great patron of art, but they lacked experience of war. The King of France's youngest son Philip, a youth of fourteen, a future Duke of Burgundy, fought at his father's side.

One reason for the French defeat may be the disunity and rivalry between Marshal d'Audrehem and Marshal de Clermont. Marshal d'Audrehem wanted to charge, while Clermont favoured more cautious tactics. This led to a furious row. When Audrehem accused Clermont of cowardice, the latter retorted: "Ha, maréchal, you are not so bold but that your horse's nose will find itself in my horse's ass."[8] Clermont was slain in a cavalry charge while Audrehem was taken prisoner.

Despite the superiority of the French in numbers, there was higher morale in the English army. None of the English commanders had more experience than Thomas de Beauchamp Earl of Warwick, commander of the vanguard, while Robert d'Ufford Earl of Suffolk and William de Montagu, second Earl of Salisbury, led the rear-guard.

It was a cruel battle in which both English and French fought ferociously and heroically. The Earl of Oxford commanded the English archers, skilfully hidden behind the hedges "to shoote at the hinder parts of the horses whereof the horses being gauld and wounded fell to tumbling with them that sate on their backs, or else turned backe and run upon them that followed after, making great slaughter upon their own masters."[9] The archers were well supported by the men-at-arms.

At a critical stage of the battle the division, commanded by the Duke of Orleans (the Dauphin), instead of attacking the hard pressed English, became demoralized and deserted the field. Then the King led 6,000 fresh troops to the assault crying, "Advance, for I will recover the day or die on the field." Had they been mounted, a French victory might have resulted, for some of the English were desperately tired and disheartened, murmuring among themselves that too many soldiers had been left to defend Gascony. Then a member of the Black Prince's staff was unwise enough to declare in a loud voice, "Alas, we are overcome", but the invincible Prince of Wales, furious at his defeatism retorted: "Thou liest, thou dastardly fellow, for thou canst not say that we can be overcome as long as I live."[10] Bringing forward his last reserve, he shouted at Chandos, "John, get forward - you shall not see me turn my back this day, but I will be ever with the foremost."[11] The Black Prince ordered his standard bearer Sir Walter Woodland to bear his standard towards the enemy. The trumpets made such a noise that even "the walles of poyters sounded with the echo thereof like a wood, in such sort that a man would have thought that the hills had bellowed out to the valleis and that the clouds had given forth a most terrible thunder."[12]

King John, surrounded by his brave French, wielded his large battle-axe with considerable skill, assisted by his son Philippe. "Beware Father, to the right, beware to the left" cried the boy as the battle-axe descended on its victims. All around dying men groaned, their blood pouring onto the earth. John was such a valuable prize if he were captured that there was tremendous competition among the English, for he would

102

command a fabulous ransom. Eventually the king yielded himself to a knight of Artois, named Denis de Morbecque, now banished the realm of France and fighting with the English. The Earl of Warwick and Lord Cobham took him to the Prince.

The redeeming feature in this medieval war was the chivalry practised by the Black Prince and noble knights like Sir James Audley, an original Knight of the Order of the Garter. Sir James had been sorely wounded and was borne in his litter by his servants to the Prince's lodging. Froissart relates that the Prince of Wales gave Audley "five hundred marks of yerely revennes", but with real generosity Audley later transferred it to the four Cheshire squires who served him. Their names were Delves of Doddington, Dutton of Dutton, Fullesburst of Bartholmly and Hawkstone of Wrinerhill. On hearing this the Prince insisted on giving Audley a second annuity of 600 marks.

The Prince, too, is seen at his best in his chivalrous reception of his prisoner, the King of France. Froissart's account differs from Le Baker's, being more romantic. We can imagine the scene, the candles in their sconces and the torches lighting up the tired faces of the combatants as the Prince with a delicate tact seated John together with his son Philippe at a table with the leading noblemen. Then the Prince personally served the king, humbly on his knees saying "he was not suffycient to syt at the table with so great a king".[13] "For God's sake, sir, make non yvell nor hevy chere, though God this day dyde not consent to followe your wyll." He assured him that his royal father, the king would treat John with much honour and consideration, so that hereafter they would be "friends...".

Froissart relates that the finest flower of French chivalry died on the Monday of the battle. Among the dead given by Baker, was Pierre Duc de Bourbon, Marshal Jean de Clermont as already mentioned, and Geoffroi de Charny, bearer of the *oriflamme*. Le Bel compared the honourable way the English treated their French captives at Poitiers with the behaviour of Germans in the flush of victory. Among the prisoners were Guillaume de Melun, Archbishop of Sens and Guichard D'Angle, Seneschal of Saintogne, who was later to serve the

Black Prince, and to gain his esteem, so that he later became tutor to his son the boy King Richard II.

It is evident that Poitiers was immensely profitable in a material sense, not only to King Edward and his son but also to the aristocracy, to the esquires and even to the archers. Froissart relates: "All suche as were there with the prince were all made ryche with honour and goodes, as well as by ransomyng of prisoners, as by wynyng of golde sylver plate, jewelles that was there found." King Edward purchased three of the Black Prince's personal captives for £20,000, while the Prince bought another fourteen on his father's behalf for £60,000. Later, too, the Earl of Warwick was able to ransom the Archbishop of Sens for the immense sum of £8,000.[14] A squire, Robert Clinton, fortunate enough to capture the Bishop of Le Mans, cleverly sold his own share to King Edward for £1,000.

Froissart relates that when the Black Prince brought his prisoners to London (May 24th 1357), the King of France rode through the city on a "whyte courser, well aparelled, and the prince on a lytell black hobbey by hym," an example of the prince's tact. It was an occasion filled with pageantry, the clang of bells, fountains spouting wine, tapestries bedecking the street, and the liveried guildsmen of the city companies taking part in the processions.[15] About midday they reached the Palace of the Savoy, newly built by Henry, Duke of Lancaster for fifty-two thousand marks (perhaps £34,000).

There King John would pass the first part of his captivity. It was far from irksome. He was often visited by King Edward and Queen Philippa, and Edward soon became attached to John of France. Later that summer he was brought to Windsor, where he enjoyed hunting and hawking in the forests with his son Philippe, while the other French prisoners remained in London, occasionally travelling to Windsor on parole to see their king. Later, after much haggling, and the first Treaty of London (January 1358), John's ransom was set at four million gold crowns.

As for John's fellow monarch, David II of Scotland, he was still held prisoner in England, but by the Treaty of Berwick

(October 1357) he was allowed his freedom on condition that a heavy ransom of 100,000 marks was paid.

XI The Black Monday Campaign

After the humiliation of Poitiers, France's fortunes reached their lowest ebb in her long history. Anarchy and chaos reigned in the land. Their King was imprisoned in England, while the Dauphin Charles, a sickly, inexperienced boy of eighteen, struggled to maintain some sort of order, though confronted by fearful problems. Far more intelligent than his father, King John, whom he did not resemble (indeed it was rumoured that his mother had been unfaithful to her husband and that he was not a Valois), the Dauphin Charles learnt statecraft through adversity. Later as Charles V, he was to reveal many estimable qualities, and French historians such as R. Delacherral[1] all agree that he possessed wisdom (*sagesse*). He is described as having "small sharp eyes, thin lips, a long thin nose, and an ill-proportioned body."[2] Christine de Pisan wrote that he was a good horseman. Partly because of his feeble health, his tastes were for learning and academic pursuits rather than martial prowess. Consequently, not the least of his achievements was to form a library of nearly 1,200 chained books in a tower of the Louvre. His intelligence was to later make him a formidable opponent of Edward III and the Black Prince.

Not only had Charles to struggle against the Third Estate of Paris and its ambitious leader Etienne Marcel, a rich draper, who was trying to demand some form of constitutional control, but he was forced to match his wits against Charles the Bad of Navarre, newly released from prison in November 1357, and scheming to set himself up as an alternative king to the Valois. On one occasion the Dauphin had to endure the humiliation and horror of seeing two of his marshals, including Jean de Clermont, son of the marshal killed at Poitiers, slain by Marcel's officers, who had succeeded in penetrating into his palace.

Small wonder if the peasants of France, groaning under the insufferable weight of fees and taxes imposed by their lords, at last revolted, blaming the nobles for their misery and the capture of King John. Then ensued the atrocities of the *Jacquerie* (May 28 1358), described by Jean Le Bel and Froissart. How the peasants hated the nobility! Froissart's sympathies are with the lords and knights, rather than the villains, and he relates how

> those evil men...violated and killed all the ladies and girls without mercy, like mad dogs...I could never bring myself to write down the horrible and shameful deeds which they did to the ladies. But, among other brutal excesses, they killed a knight, put him on a spit...and roasted him before the lady and her children. After about a dozen of them had violated the lady, they tried to force her and the children to eat the knight's flesh before putting them cruelly to death.

Froissart takes this story from the antecedent chronicle of Le Bel, and the latter was not given to exaggeration. The worst excesses occurred in the Beauvais, in Brie, on the Marne, in Valois and round Soissons. Regarding the leaders of *The Jacquerie* as useful allies, Etienne Marcel tried to employ them as an auxiliary army, but he later met a violent death, killed by the guards of St. Antoine in Paris. Earlier the Dauphin, now the Regent, had been forced to flee from Paris, but returned on horseback at the beginning of August to the Louvre to the cheers of the volatile Parisians. The revolt of *The Jacquerie*, a futile insurrection, was ruthlessly put down, and about 20,000 wretched peasants killed and the countryside became a desert.

While France passed through these terrible sufferings, and the Regent Charles learnt through his bitter experiences and desperation the necessity of patience and cunning in dealing with his ruthless enemies, his father remained Edward's favoured prisoner. Naturally wanting to regain his freedom, John nevertheless had a comparatively good time, maintaining an astrologer and "a King of minstrels" with an orchestra, holding an occasional cockfight, selling horses and wine he had received as gifts, and content enough among his dogs and falcons.

The negotiations for John's release were all the more wearisome and protracted owing to Edward's harsh demands. While John's ransom was fixed at 4 million gold crowns, Edward wanted not only the sovereignty of Guyenne, together with Poitou, Ponthieu and other regions already agreed to by the Dauphin, but Anjou, Maine and Normandy, the Pas-de-Calais and the overlordship of Brittany. If these conditions were agreed to, Edward was ready to waive his title of King of England and France. King John, no doubt under pressure, yielded to the new agreement of 1359, but the Dauphin with his political sense refused to accept these humiliating conditions, and his decision was supported by his councillors. In their defiance they maintained the treaty "was displeasing to all the people of France". War was preferable to surrender.

Accusing the French of perfidy, Edward organized an immense army of 30,000 men, 6,000 of whom were men-at-arms. Most of the nobility were eager to serve on this campaign, and men of humble rank, tempted by the decisive Battle of Poitiers and visions of the rich plunder in store. All Edward's sons were there, the noble Black Prince, Lionel of Clarence (an unlucky title), John of Gaunt, and Edmund of Langley. Only his younger son Thomas of Woodstock, then aged four, remained at home. When one reflects that this campaign was for the most part a failure, it is evident that the King made two serious mistakes and miscalculations. Perhaps after Poitiers he was over-confident. He spoke of total victory and of a peace rebounding to his honour. His great ambition was to be crowned King of France at Rheims, the traditional place of consecration. In harbouring his lofty idea, Edward was surely indulging in an illusion. Did he seriously think that the inhabitants of Rheims would hasten to adhere to his cause? To delude himself that they would open their gates to their legitimate sovereign as he conceived himself, might satisfy his vanity, but it was unrealistic. He almost certainly envisaged an easy victory and no prolonged resistance. In thinking so, he made the mistake of underestimating the quality of his enemy, the Regent Charles. Indeed he had no means of knowing the ability, as yet largely hidden, of this prince. Nor was he aware of the new nationalism rising in the hearts of Frenchmen, smarting with injured pride and humiliation.

A massive expedition required many months of preparation, but it seems surprising that Edward, such an experienced warrior, should embark on a winter campaign, instead of a spring one. He did not land at Calais until October 28th (1359). Froissart relates

> that the great English lords and men of substance took with them tents of various sizes, mills for grinding corn, ovens for baking, forges for shoeing the horses...

Eight thousand wagons were required for carrying all these necessities. The King and his nobles evidently intended to enjoy themselves when their leisure permitted, for Edward had for his personal use, thirty mounted falconers, many birds, together with sixty couples of large hounds with which he intended to hunt or go wild-fowling.

Before setting out on his *chevauchée* from Calais, on Monday November 4th by way of Artois and Champagne to Rheims, Edward was joined by some *routiers*, including the renowned Robert Knollys, a born leader and soldier but an unscrupulous brigand. These *routiers* consisted of English and Gascon deserters, lawless French, only too ready to terrorize parts of the country, and German mercenaries hoping for plunder and adventure.[3] The invading army was divided into three bodies, lead by the King himself, the Black Prince and the Duke of Lancaster. So they slowly advanced, overladen with baggage, burning and plundering as was customary in a *chevauchée*. Edward's star, so long in the ascendant, deserted him at this juncture. Rain fell monotonously, and provisions in a country ravaged by war were scarce. Edward hoped for a pitched battle like Crécy or Poitiers, but the strategy of the Regent Charles was to avoid pitched battles, and instead attempt to exhaust the enemy by fortifying the towns and castles to withstand attack. Edward's misjudgement was to cost him dear at Rheims. The Dauphin Charles had given instructions to the captain of the garrison, Gaucher de Châtillon, to strengthen the city walls. Fired by his enthusiasm the inhabitants, loyal to their Valois rulers, manfully resisted. In the surrounding country everything was destroyed that might assist the enemy. The Archbishop Jean de Craon had resourcefully stored provisions in the city, prepared for a long siege.

For Edward, the sight of the monastery of St. Thierry at the gates of Rheims being devoured by fire, was exasperating for he had intended to make it his headquarters.

It is curious to record that among those serving in the English army, in the household of Lionel of Clarence, was Geoffrey Chaucer, then aged twenty. His experiences were to give him a marked aversion for warfare. While engaged on a foraging expedition he was captured by the French, and King Edward shared in his ransoming, paying £16.

Unable to provoke the French to pitched battle, and mindful that his troops were suffering hardship and hunger, deprived of provisions in the pitiless rain and freezing snow of the winter (1359-1360), Edward was forced to raise the siege after nearly two months. He had abandoned all hope of being crowned in Rheims. Heading south for the rich land of Burgundy, burning and looting as he advanced, until the then Duke of Burgundy, Philip de Rouvre bought him off for 200,000 moutons d'or (£33,000). In Tonnerre in Upper Burgundy, the English consoled themselves, drinking 3,000 butts of wine. The King then turned towards Paris. On the way, he heard that the French, on March 15th 1360, had taken advantage of his absence from his kingdom to burn and sack the port of Winchelsea, at the same time raping some terrified ladies in St. Thomas's Church. Deeply mortified and giving way to one of his Plantagenet rages, Edward set fire to many villages in the neighbourhood of Paris.[4]

Edward wanted to provoke the French to come out from Paris to attack him, but the Regent Charles, no ardent knight like his father, was too wily to be tempted. The King of England decided to retreat. Near Chartres, however, one of the most terrible disasters befell Edward's troops. It occurred on 'Black Monday' April 13th, "a foul dark day of mist and of hail, so bitter cold that sitting on horseback many died". All the French and English chroniclers, including Jean de Venette describe it. And a fortnight later, while in the valley of the Loire, a thunderstorm burst over the terrified troops as they wended their way across the stony heaths beyond Chartres - the hailstones were as big as pigeons' eggs and the lightning may have killed more knights in armour than fell at Crécy and Poitiers.[5] These fearsome events made an enormous impact on King Edward's mind. In his own way he was very religious, and it was a superstitious age. He undoubtedly thought that the calamity that had befallen his men was a sign of God's anger. It inclined him towards peace, causing Edward "to turn towards the church of Our Lady at Chartres and devoutly vow to the Virgin that he would accept terms of peace".

It was now when the war-wearied French longed for peace, that an intermediary, the Abbot of Cluny, arrived at Edward's headquarters with peace proposals at the end of April.[6] In the king's entourage was his own cousin, Henry of Grosmont Duke of Lancaster, an eloquent advocate for peace. He wisely contended that Edward should accept these proposals, "for my Lord," he urged, "we could lose more in one day than we have gained in twenty years."[7]

On May 1st 1360, negotiations were opened at the little village of Brétigny, near Chartres. The provisional Treaty of Brétigny signed a week later, contained a maze of complicated clauses in 39 articles. Its important points were Edward's renunciation of his claim to the French throne and his overlordships of Normandy, Brittany and Flanders, Anjou, Maine and Touraine. However, he was very amply compensated by the unconditional cession of the whole of Aquitaine, a huge state comprising one third of France, and of many other places, including Limousin, Poitou, Périgord, Rouergne, and the cities of Limoges, Poitiers and Angoulême and La Rochelle, the centre of the European salt trade. An important provision was King John's ransom, settled at three million gold crowns (£500,000) in six instalments. On payment of the first instalment, provided the King of France left three of his sons as hostages, he was to be allowed to return home. France was to renounce the alliance with Scotland, and England her alliance with the Flemish.

To regain his freedom and to obtain the necessary ransom money, King John was prepared to sell his eleven year old daughter Isabelle of Valois to the heir of Galeazzo Visconti, a rich Milanese nobleman. A contemporary Italian Matteo Villani, incredulous and contemptuous, wrote: "who could imagine, considering the greatness of the crown of France, that the wearer of that crown should be reduced to such straite as virtually to sell his own flesh at auction?"[8] The Italian chroniclers admiringly refer to the marriage on October 8th 1360 celebrated with true magnificence in Milan. She was to die at the age of twenty-three after giving birth to several children.

On October 24th 1360, the Treaty of Brétigny was ratified at Calais, and again when Edward III opened Parliament during February 1361, after a grand procession to Westminster Abbey, where Simon of Islip, Archbishop of Canterbury, celebrated High Mass. The Treaty, so impressive to Edward's contemporaries, was only partially successful. Edward refused to abandon his title to the French crown, on the pretexts that the French so far had not yet handed over the towns and territories agreed to by the Treaty, and they were delaying sending the promised ransom money for the release of King John. If Edward is to be regarded as a statesman, he ought to have adhered to the Treaty, for there were sufficient safeguards. The French diplomats then refused to make a unilateral surrender of King John's suzerainty over Aquitaine. To render the vital question of ultimate sovereignty thoroughly uncertain, did not bring lasting peace.

Meanwhile King John had been waiting in custody at Calais until October 24th, when 400,000 gold crowns, two thirds of his ransom money, had been paid. The hostages, including the Duke of Anjou and other sons of King John, and a nobleman Enguerrard de Coucy, destined to become Edward III's son-in-law, sailed for England. Since he genuinely liked John, Edward entertained him and his son Philippe, created Duke of Burgundy in 1364, at a banquet. It is said that Philippe, enraged because the master butler served King Edward before his father, rose from the table, striking him with the cry: "Where did you learn to serve the King of England before the King of France when they are at the same table?" Whereupon Edward tactfully remarked, "Verily, cousin, you are Philip the Bold."[9] Much to the annoyance of his father, the Duke of Anjou, one of the hostages, broke parole in England, returning to Boulogne to see his wife, with whom he was much in love. Consequently King John, an honourable man, felt bound to return to England, for he considered his son's act, one of betrayal, reflecting on his crown. It is possible there were other reasons, John's inner awareness of his inadequacy to deal with the complicated affairs of state or hoping, perhaps, as he enjoyed agreeable relations with King Edward, to persuade him to reduce the remainder of his ransom unpaid. Possibly John had enjoyed himself sufficiently in England, putting his personal desires before the desperate needs of his country. Jean de Venette, hostile to the monarchy, considered that he returned to his pleasant captivity for reasons of pleasure.

John II returned to England in early January 1364, saying "If good faith were banished from the rest of the earth, it should still be found in the hearts and mouths of Kings." He was not sorry to return to the urbane attractions of the palace of the Savoy, but within three months he had sickened of an unknown disease and was dead. The sanitary conditions in London were very primitive at this period. Possibly, too, his too lavish life-style, the rich food and over-indulgence in wines had contributed to his comparatively early death, on April 4th, at the age of forty-four.

Edward genuinely grieved for the death of his brother monarch, gave him a splendid requiem at St. Paul's, and his remains were later returned to France for burial at St. Denis.

Despite his infidelities, Edward III was always devoted to Queen Philippa, remaining intimate with her. She bore her husband twelve children, seven sons and five daughters, but three died in infancy or childhood. Unlike earlier Plantagenet kings, such as Henry II, Edward did not quarrel with his sons, indeed his generosity towards them must be commended. One of his main concerns was to arrange advantageous, dynastic marriages for them and his daughters. However, he sometimes promoted alliances for his daughters expedient to his own political interests, though he carefully avoided thwarting their inclinations.[1]

Edward's favourite daughter was undoubtedly his eldest, Isabella, born at Woodstock, June 16th 1332. Unfortunately, he treated her with too much indulgence, pampering and spoiling her. In her infancy, a tailor, John Bromley, was appointed to serve her. At her first public appearance she was dressed in a costly robe of Lucca silk, edged with rich furs, while her mother Queen Philippa, as was customary, lay upon her state-bed, lavishly dressed in a robe of red and purple velvet embroidered with pearls, to receive the compliments of the court.[2]

Her father planned to marry Isabella, in infancy, to Pedro, afterwards surnamed 'the Cruel', eldest son of Alphonso, King of Castile, but fortunately for Isabella, nothing came of the proposed match, and Pedro became the suitor of her younger sister Joanna. Then Edward, for whom the Flemish alliance was of significant importance in his prosecution of the war, tried hard to promote a marriage between Isabella and young Louis Earl of Flanders, but Louis, encouraged by Philip VI of France, was ardently in love with a Brabant princess and jilted Isabella, despite the advanced negotiations. Then the capricious girl of twenty-one, in her turn, jilted her next suitor, a distinguished Gascon nobleman named Bernard Ezi, Lord of Albret, for the marriage was suddenly broken off before consummation. The broken-hearted bridegroom is said to have retired to a monastery. Knowing his daughter's inconstant nature, Edward had stipulated in the marriage contract that if Bernard were to die or any other circumstances were to occur to prevent its completion, not only the dowry but the costly bridal dresses should be returned to the princess. So, he encouraged her compulsive extravagance, for she even pawned her jewels on occasions, being unable to pay the wages of her servants and having to borrow from her father. It is fair to say, however, that she often bestowed alms on the poor when she travelled.

Among the grants of land given her by her father, were the Castle of Carisbrook in the Isle of Wight and the manor of Walsham in the east riding of Yorkshire. When Edward granted to her the lands and custody of young Edmund Mortimer, Earl of March (afterwards married to Philippa, daughter of her brother Lionel Duke of Clarence), Isabella made a mercenary agreement with her ward's mother, whereby she disposed of the grant for 1,000 marks, stipulating that if the money to be used for Mortimer's maintenance and education was not paid on the day due, she would insist on a double payment.

Isabella's fate was very much affected by King John of France's imprisonment in England. A clause in the Treaty of Brétigny had stipulated that twenty-five members of the French nobility, including Enguerrand de Coucy, Lord of Coucy, la Fère et Oise, should be sent over to England as hostages. Isabella now over thirty, fell in love with the accomplished nobleman, not only a brave soldier, but an elegant dancer with a fine voice, very pleasing to her father. A great success at Edward's court, he was much admired for his gallantry by the ladies. When Isabella, then thirty-three, married her suitor on July 27th, 1365, in Windsor Castle, the best minstrels in the country performed. It was a resplendent occasion, for Edward, Philippa and their sons all contributed to the purchase of some magnificent jewels as a wedding present for the bride, costing altogether £2,370.13s.4d. Edward's present to his son-in-law was to release him as a hostage without payment of his ransom, as he also restored to him all the manors and lands in Yorkshire, Lancashire and Cumberland owned by his family, giving him the English title of Earl of Bedford. The King sensed that Enguerrand would be an important ally, for his name was greatly esteemed in France.

Isabella never cared to remain for long on her husband's vast estate of Coucy-le-Château in Picardy. Her nostalgia for her father's gay court was so strong that when her husband embarked on a military expedition, she would return immediately to England. Both Princess Isabella and her mother might well have been affected by the Statute of Treasons (1352). This important Act of Parliament defined treason as a specific crime. Anybody adjudged guilty of encompassing the death of the King, his Chancellor or judges, or violating Edward III's Queen or his eldest daughter (Isabella) would be committing treason. It applied also to levying war against the King in his realm.

Edward and Philippa's second daughter Joanna was born at the Tower of London, a very pathetic character because of her early death from the pestilence at Loremo, a small village near Bordeaux. However, she was spared a probable unhappy marriage with Pedro, son of Alphonso King of Castile, as already recorded.

Joanna was Queen Philippa's favourite child, and she was fortunate, at least in her infancy, when her training and education were entrusted to Mary of St. Pol,[3] widowed Countess of Pembroke, a learned lady, who founded Pembroke College, Cambridge. Joanna was very fond of embroidery. The little, bronze image of 'Joanna of the Tower' can be seen today on the south side of Edward III's tomb of Purbeck marble in Westminster Abbey, next to the bronze images of the Black Prince and Lionel of Clarence.

Mary, Joanna's younger sister, born at Waltham, near Winchester, in 1344, was married to Duke John IV of Brittany to further her father's French dynastic policy, but her parents were desolate when Mary died aged seventeen soon after her marriage.[4]

Edward's fifth daughter, born at Windsor during July 1346, named Margaret, made a love match with John, son and heir of Lawrence Hastings, Earl of Pembroke. After his father's death (1348), the infant became a ward of Edward III. It is curious that in early life, he was so intimately connected with the King, since his mother, Agnes, was one of the daughters of Roger Mortimer, Earl of March, the paramour of Queen Isabella. At court, a staunch friendship matured between John Hastings and Edmund of Langley, Edward's younger son, and they later served abroad together, in various campaigns.

It was natural enough that Margaret should form an attachment for her brother's friend, one that was mutual and warmly approved of by her father. Edward, at heart a family man, and cursing the ill fate that attended the marriage of two of his daughters to foreign potentates, relished the thought that Margaret, married to Hastings, would remain near him at court.

In 1359, there were joyful scenes when two marriages were celebrated on the same day, that of her brother Lionel, to Elizabeth de Burgh, heiress daughter of the Earl of Ulster, and Margaret's wedding to John Hastings, Earl of Pembroke. Lionel's first marriage to Elizabeth de Burgh was advantageous to King Edward, not only because his bride was well endowed, but because through her, he became the leading Irish landowner, possessing the important Clare inheritance in Ulster and Connaught. Both brides were lavishly bedecked with pearls costing £16.13s.4d.[5] and Margaret displayed a coronet of gems, a present from her father. Edward III was very fond of Pembroke, whose military career was very distinguished, so that in 1372, the King conferred on him the lieutenancy of Aquitaine. Froissart commemorates his exploits, especially in Bretagne and Gascony. However, he was intercepted off Rochelle by a Spanish fleet allied with France, and was forced to languish in prison for two years and to be treated harshly. Edward would refer to Pembroke as John, "my fair son", and was very sad when the nobleman in his twenty-eighth year died at Arras. Pembroke was then a widower, for his first wife Margaret, had died in 1361, after only two years of marriage.

In the later medieval age, marriages were generally consummated at 14 or 15, although contracts of marriage between the highborn were sometimes arranged either in infancy or early childhood. Such was the betrothal between Robert de Vere, aged ten, later favourite of Richard II, and Philippa de Coucy, only four, younger daughter of Princess Isabella and Enguerrand de Coucy.

Edward's Queen Philippa was always virtuous, but the level of morality at Edward's court was far from high. At tournaments, people were scandalized by the presence of ladies of easy virtue, exhibiting a "scurrilous wantonness",[6] dressed in divers and wonderful male attire as if they were part of the tourney.

> They wore divers and wonderful male attire, particoloured tunics, and their short capes contained daggers in pouches. Not to be outdone they rode fine coursers and palfreys.

Women were much criticized for plucking eyebrows and the hairline, because it was considered God did not intend it.

Christine de Pisan, the daughter of Thomas of Pisano, the French King Charles V's physician-astrologer, was almost certainly the only medieval woman to earn her living by the pen. She eulogizes Charles V in her biography, much admiring him. Born in 1364, she was only thirteen when Edward III died, and throughout her literary career a passionate champion of women's rights.

Edward III was less cultured than Philippa, but he maintained a splendid royal court. Characteristic of him was his court orchestra, five trumpeters, one citoles (guitarist), five pipes, one tabouretter, two clarion-players, one neckener (kettle-drum), one fiddler and three waits or singers. In times of war, this orchestra became a military band.[7] As a patron, however, he was outshone by Philippa, who introduced from Hainault a higher civilized standard, and a real feeling for literature. She was responsible as an early patron of Jean Froissart for bringing him to Edward's court and in her patronage of Chaucer, her influence was by no means negligible. Philippa appointed Froissart a clerk of her royal chapel, taking him into her service as "ditteur", reader or poet laureate. He never forgot his benefactress. The most important of his foreign patrons was probably Wenceslas King of Bohemia, his collaborator. One defect in the chronicler's character cannot lightly be forgiven, his proneness to transfer his allegiance or even to desert his patron when ill fortune befell him.

Philippa showed shrewdness in not surrounding herself with aliens, like Eleanor of Provence, Henry III's queen. A strong personality with determined opinion, she was instrumental in getting women to attend the elaborate court banquets.

Our picture of Edward the Black Prince is so vivid with his prowess as a warrior at Crécy, Poitiers and Nájera that we are apt to overlook his achievements in peace time or his rôle as husband. He is still a legend, born to greatness, and created Earl of Chester at the age of three and later Earl of Cornwall. He was knighted during the Crécy campaign at Saint-Vaast-de-la-Hougue, in Normandy, at the age of sixteen. Before his marriage to the beautiful Princess Joan of Kent, the Prince fathered one or two illegitimate sons, but he married late at the age of thirty. One of his first biographers wrote: "The most heroick Prince of Wales, soften'd with peace, was now captive in love, being smitten with the charms of Joan, Countess of Kent."[8] Since the Prince and Joan were related within the second and third degree, having the same great-grandfather Edward I, it was necessary to obtain a dispensation from Pope Innocent VI at Avignon, and this was soon forthcoming.

It is probable that Edward and Philippa did not at first approve of this much married lady as a bride for their son, but they were present together with John of Gaunt, Edmund of Langley, Joan, Queen of Scotland (David Bruce's estranged wife), and the Prince's sister Isabella, when their marriage was solemnized in Windsor Castle on October 10th 1361. There is absolutely no evidence that Edward III quarrelled with his son after the marriage. The Prince, however, seems to have kept this affair concealed from his parents for some time.

Edward the Black Prince was a man of action, but when granted the principality of Aquitaine, he showed a lack of sensibility and an impatience in dealing with diplomatic niceties relating to his Gascon subjects. He revealed early on that if he had ever to succeed his father as king, he would lack the necessary statesmanship to deal with difficult circumstances.

Shakespeare's description of the Black Prince in the memorable words of Edmund of Langley (Duke of York), only provides part of the picture:

> In war, was never lion rag'd more fierce
> In peace was never gentle lamb more mild
> Than was that young and princely gentleman.[9]

As the owner of estates in Restormel Castle, Cornwall, in Kennington and at Berkhamsted in Hertfordshire, where the Prince and Princess of Wales were visited by his father and mother, he was loyally and competently served by his staff, but he lacked administrative ability. One of his faults was a compulsive extravagance, particularly his expenditure on tournaments and lavish purchases of jewellery, and Joan failed to exercise any restraint on her husband.

Edward III's third son, a genial giant, Lionel of Antwerp, created Duke of Clarence, made no real mark on history, but the King sent him to Ireland, where he became, in effect, his viceroy. Lionel became the most important Irish landowner, for he inherited through his first wife Elizabeth, the vast Clare estates in Ulster and Connaught. Edward, too preoccupied elsewhere, had little time for Ireland, nor did he reveal any vision, like his grandson Richard II. Elizabeth died early, after giving Lionel a daughter Philippa, but he married again, Violante Visconti, the thirteen-year-old daughter of a very wealthy Italian, Galeazzo Visconti II,[10] ruler of the ancient city of Pavia, and brother of Bernabò, a lustful tyrant. Humphrey de Bohun was entrusted by Edward III with the negotiations and sent to Pavia during April 1368, but it took two years to complete them, after a treaty signed at Windsor.

Never was a more magnificent wedding banquet provided by a grateful father, well satisfied that his daughter was marrying the son of a king. However, it did not lack vulgar ostentation. It was high summer and the banquet was held in the

120

open courtyard of a palace. The table was replete with all kinds of delicacies, sucking pig, veal, trout, quail, partridge, duck, heron, chicken, rabbit, eels and sturgeon, consisting altogether of eighteen courses. Meanwhile the fortunate bridegroom looked on, perhaps slightly bewildered, as he was ceremonially offered great rolls of silk and brocade from the looms of Milan, the richest city in Lombardy, and other lavish presents, including the exquisite Milanese armour, all bearing the crest of Visconti and Clarence.[11] Geoffrey Chaucer was among the guests at the same table as Lionel.

Nothing loath to assume the agreeable life of an Italian nobleman, after his marriage, Lionel of Clarence left for his new estates in Piedmont. His intemperance almost certainly shortened his life, for whilst visiting Violante's family at Pavia, he succumbed to a fever from which he died, aged almost thirty. The English, as was inevitable, suspected that he had been poisoned, but it is almost certainly untrue.

Edward was more fortunate in his dynastic projects when his fourth son, born at Ghent in 1340, known as John of Gaunt, married firstly Blanche, daughter of Henry of Grosmont, Duke of Lancaster, a great heiress. Froissart described Blanche, so loved by her contemporaries: "Gay and glad she was, fresh and sportive, sweet simple and of humble semblance, the fair lady whom men called Blanche." She died too early, aged about twenty-two, commemorated by Chaucer in the *Book of the Duchess*. His father-in-law had already died, so John of Gaunt acquired the largest groups of territories in England next to the Crown itself, the Duchy of Lancaster and the Earldoms of Leicester, Lincoln and Derby, and manors all over England and Wales, making him the richest landowner in England. For Edward III, Gaunt's vast inheritance must have seemed a triumph, but for a subject to acquire so much wealth made him, or his son and heir, a potential menace to the Crown in the future. John of Gaunt was not only energetic, but very ambitious, a poor soldier, but able diplomat. His second marriage during 1371 to a Spanish Princess Constance, daughter of Pedro the Cruel of Castile, intensified his ambitions, for he wished to wear a crown himself, dreaming of being crowned as the husband of the Queen of Castile and Leon in the Cathedral of Burgos. This was no love match, unlike his elder brother's, the Prince of Wales.

Edward III's plan to marry his fifth son, Edmund of Langley, to Margaret, the only child of Louis de Male and heiress to Flanders, Artois and imperial Burgundy, in an attempt to revive the Anglo-Flemish coalition in the 1360s, was thwarted by the scheming of Charles V of France. He adroitly persuaded the pro-French Pope Urban V, to refuse to grant a dispensation, and later, in 1369, succeeded in marrying Margaret to his brother Philip le Hardi, Duke of Burgundy. Edmund espoused a sister of Constance of Castile as his first wife, thus implementing King Edward's policy in Spain. His youngest son, Thomas of Woodstock, destined to be smothered in a feather bed in Calais during the reign of Edward's grandson, made an advantageous marriage with Eleanor, one of the co-heiress daughters of Humphrey de Bohun, Earl of Hereford and Constable of England. On the whole, Edward's marriage policy was a success, shrewdly balanced, but the early death of at least two of his daughters and one of his sons, afflicted him sorely.

XIII A Great Builder

As a builder, Edward III may be aptly compared with Henry III. Both Plantagenet kings succeeded to the throne in boyhood, and Edward, Henry's great-grandson, was to reign almost as long. While Henry had little flair for dealing with the complicated pattern of political events, and had no martial ability whatsoever, Edward for many years was a highly successful ruler. Henry's patronage of the arts and immense importance as a builder surely compensated him for his failure in kingcraft, while Edward's building activities at Eltham, Windsor and many other places aptly expressed one aspect of his ability as a ruler.[1] Edward's building at Windsor, the centre of his court, expressed a concept of kingship long before Le Roi Soleil's Versailles. Edward's own grandfather, Edward 'Longshanks', may also be called a great builder, particularly of those eight castles in North Wales costing £80,000 spent between 1277-1304, and his reconstruction of the Tower of London costing over £20,000 between 1275-1285. Nor must we omit Vale Royal Abbey in Cheshire, so magnificently conceived, but not destined to endure. Of the later Plantagenet kings, the Yorkist, Edward IV, deserves the appellation of a great builder, especially for his work at Windsor, and the beauties of the Great Hall at Eltham, so lovingly preserved today.

The growing nationalism and patriotism stimulated by the long wars with France found expression in the great architecture and art of the fourteenth century. Crécy, for instance, inspired one of the commanders Lord Bradeston to commission the important Crécy window, so beautiful a feature of Gloucester Cathedral. The stained glass at the base curiously enough depicts a medieval golfer. What made it possible for the great rebuilding work to come about was the wealth brought about by the constant stream of pilgrims to Gloucester Cathedral ardent to venerate the shrine of Edward II. William de Ramsey was responsible for refashioning the old Norman choir by adopting a peculiarly English style of architecture known as the Perpendicular. His massive reconstruction took place over ten years during the decade 1330-1340.[2] It might be described as England's unique contribution to the art of architecture.

Today the Museum of London has begun massive excavations on the sites of two royal palaces. "The Rosary" belonged to the King's father Edward II. It stood on the left bank of the Thames, a large moated building about 80 yards square where Edward could relax with his favourite, Piers Gaveston - at least up to 1312. The moated Manor House at Rotherhithe on the Thames was built for Edward III; one of the group of royal residences along the Thames favoured by the King. It is known that Edward began his major works in the manor in February 1353.[3] Eight years later by September 1361 £1,200 was spent on a hall, kitchen, various chambers, a wharf linked to the main building by a bridge over the moat, a gatehouse, a garden and various interior fixtures such as a fireplace, and a candelabra and tiling for walls and floors.[4]

In his architectural projects, Edward was much influenced by William of Wykeham, born of poor parents in 1324, although his mother had gentle blood in her veins.[5] Wykeham is a village lying halfway between Fareham and Bishop's Waltham in Hampshire. It was in the autumn of 1356 that Wykeham was appointed as Surveyor of the works at Windsor Castle, and he advised Edward III to demolish all the building to the east of the new keep or Round Table, and to build instead another ward or bailey for himself and his court, retaining the buildings east of the new keep for the knights of the Garter. It was part of Wykeham's work to impress three hundred diggers and stone-hewers into the royal service. Froissart bears testimony to Wykeham's rise to power:

> At this time there reigned a priest in England called Sir William de Wican and this Sir William de Wican was so much in favour with the King of England, that by him everything was done, and without him they did nothing.

He is said to have inscribed on an inner wall at Windsor these words, "This made Wickham". Those envious of Wykeham hastened to report this to the King, making it seem that Wykeham was attempting to assume the glory due to the sovereign, but he assured Edward the real meaning of the words was not that Wykeham had made the castle, but that the castle had made Wykeham.[6] He was given enormous supervisory powers. On July 10th 1359 the King's "beloved clerk" William of Wykeham was appointed "Chief Keeper and Surveyor" of the castles of Windsor, Leeds, Dover and Hadleigh and of the Manors of Old and New Windsor, Wychemere, Eton, Easthampstead, Guildford, Sheen, Eltham and King's Langley.

Another castle, now no more, closely associated with Wykeham, was Queenborough in the Isle of Sheppey, Kent. Edward III paid his first visit to Queenborough in the spring of 1361, the first of many visits to this castle, named in honour of Queen Philippa. According to William of Wykeham's accounts for the seven months March-November 1361, as much as £1,500 was spent on Queenborough, rising to over £4,000 from November 1363-November 1364. It cost altogether £25,000. Especially costly were the materials used, such as Stapleton and Reigate Stone.[7]

Queenborough was primarily designed for coastal defence against possible French raiders, and particularly for the defence of the Thames Estuary. In this medieval age when artillery was first used, we hear of guns at Queenborough (according to Professor Tout), and "stone-throwing engines" are certainly mentioned in the accounts.

Edward was keenly interested in clocks and Queenborough Castle, together with Westminster, Windsor and King's Langley, were the earliest castles where the records show there were striking clocks, weight-driven and mechanical. It was the duty of the royal *horologiarius* Keeper of the King's Club at Westminster named John Lincoln, to travel to Queenborough if something went wrong with its works.

Queenborough is reputed to have affinities with Frederick II's thirteenth-century Castel del Monte in Apulia, southern Italy,[8] an octagonal building with eight towers which were also octagonal. Unfortunately Queenborough was destroyed by Parliament during the Civil War and we lack architectural details, though a sixteenth-century ground plan and a seventeenth-century drawing have survived.

Queenborough became one of Edward's favourite castles as he grew older, and he would often visit it by water, travelling in the royal barge from Hadleigh on the opposite Essex shore. Hadleigh Castle was also intended as a work of defence by the King to prevent French raids on the coast.

Edward achieved much at Westminster, completing the building of St. Stephen's Chapel between 1331-1363. There, he had himself portrayed with Philippa, together with nine of their children, forty servers and thirty-six knights. Actually the building of St. Stephen's Chapel took fifty-six years, the work of three kings, Edward I, Edward II and Edward III. By 1345 the upper walls were complete and Master William of Hurley, together with the masons under the direction of Master William of Ramsey, were setting up the canopied niches, intended to house figures of angels[9] standing between the main windows. The work of glazing the Chapel, begun in 1349, was undertaken by a glazier called John of Brampton, whose task was to buy glass in London, Shropshire and Staffordshire.

Two favourite palaces of King Edward were Eltham and Sheen. Anthony Bek, Bishop of Durham, had originally granted the reversion of Eltham to Edward of Caernavon, when Prince of Wales, and for some time it remained in the hands of Queen Isabella, until it reverted to her eldest son. Edward's building work took place mostly over nine years between 1350-1359, costing altogether over £2,237. New chambers and a new drawbridge were constructed, and other improvements included a new kitchen, roasting-house, saucery, larder and oratory. One refinement the King added to Eltham, was a bathhouse paved with stone, with hot water piped direct into the tub. At Westminster, in 1361, Robert Foundon was paid 56s.8d for installing two large taps for Edward's bath-tub. There were, however, no personal latrines in the age of Edward III, since water-closets first appeared in the late sixteenth century.

Both Eltham and Sheen had lovely gardens. After 1358 Sheen became one of Edward's most favoured manors, and he spent much time there, dying there in June 1377. He spent what was then the large sum of £2,000 on the manor, as is recorded in William of Wykeham's accounts between October 1358-November 1361. Not only was money spent on the building, but also on the garden, the fish ponds and the planting of vines. The accounts of Bernard Cook, Clerk of the Works at Sheen, Eltham and Rotherhithe, show that a total of £556 was spent upon Sheen during one year, November 1362-November 1363. This included the wages of ditchers working on the moat. In 1374 - towards the end of Edward's life - eight feet of glass, depicting The Last Judgement, was purchased from John Brampton of London and set in the facade of the great chapel. We also hear of a new belfry being made for the clock.

Leeds Castle, near Maidstone, loveliest of places, beloved by Plantagenet kings and their queens, had belonged to Edward's mother, Queen Isabella, after she had gained power in 1327, but ten years later she had been compelled to surrender it to Edward. Much to her fury during April 1321 on a journey to Canterbury she had been refused admittance to Leeds Castle by Lady Badlesmere and a kinsman of her husband Bartholomew Burghersh. Despite her disgrace, her son always treated her with scrupulous fairness, for she was later allowed to hold Leeds until her death (1358). Edward spent about £1,500 on the castle, particularly on the dilapidated walls and on the beautiful park. From July 1359 William of Wykeham was appointed principal Keeper and Surveyor of Leeds Castle, and his accounts show that £246.11s.8½d was spent upon Leeds for just over two years between March 25th 1359 and 12 April 1361.

Woodstock in Oxfordshire, was one of the most ancient of royal palaces, and a favourite residence of Henry II, who kept his mistress there, the fair Rosamund. Edward III was attached to Woodstock because of the hunting, and three at least of Queen Philippa's children, Edward later the Black Prince, Isabella, and Thomas of Woodstock, her youngest son, were born there. Repairs and a new chamber to replace Rosamund's Chamber cost £513.2s.3d between 1364-1367.

It was natural for Edward III to be fond of his father's favourite manor of King's Langley, and the records show that the King spent the large sum of £2,300 on the residence and on the Dominican priory between 1366-1377. It is known that the principal mason employed throughout the works was John Smith. About 1368 he was paid £4 for making at Taskwork one chapel for the infirmary, one pulpit for *le Freytour* with one oriel and three fireplaces.[10] One of Edward's favourite clocks was set up in the belfry in 1368 but the great bell which Master John Belleyetere had cast for it must have occasioned much trouble for those who had to transport it from Westminster to Langley.

The manor-house at Kennington, near Lambeth, is more associated with the Black Prince than with his father, and the boy king Richard II was to inherit Kennington from his father.

Of Edward's two personal foundations, the Cistercian St. Mary's Eastminster and his Dominican nunnery at Dartford in Kent, nothing remains today. The nunnery at Dartford was founded to fulfil a vow of his father.

In the drawing-room of the Deanery of Windsor Castle there is an interesting medieval portrait of Edward III, and visitors to York Minster can see him in the windows of the Lady Chapel between St. Peter and St. Samuel. The background is replete with garters. The entrance to the cloister of St. George (1351) is one of the earliest Perpendicular buildings in England.

While Edward pursued his martial glories overseas, we can but wonder at the creative ability of England's craftsmen. His reign saw the flowering of the Perpendicular style. It was indeed a marvellous period of the finest ecclesiastical architecture. We think of the resplendent Percy tomb at Beverley, Yorkshire, the west front and nave of York Minster, and the wonderful decorated nave of the Cathedral at Exeter. Lastly must be mentioned the construction of a great part of the Tower wharf, in the Tower of London during Edward's reign, surviving to some extent to the present day. Robert Yevele, brother of the more famous Henry, designed architectural improvements to the Bloody Tower, then known as the Garden Tower because it led into the gardens of the Queen's House.

Edward never really recovered from the disastrous winter campaign of 1359-1360 when men and horses died on the terrible Black Monday. It would seem that the tremendous energy, so characteristic of his earlier years, had sapped. He became far less active, neglecting his administrative work, but indulging in his favourite pastime of hunting at Richmond, Havering and Eltham. His health was failing and now aged fifty he suffered intensely from the cold. Almost certainly he was drinking.

About 1364 we hear for the first time of a new mistress, Alice Perrers. Whether Queen Philippa objected to her installation as a maid of her bedchamber is not known, but she cannot have approved of her. It is untrue that there had been no sexual scandals in the King's earlier life as already related, but most of his amatory affairs were light rather than serious. The Victorians, of course, condemn Edward for his immorality, but after Philippa's death in 1369, the lonely Edward needed a woman of strong character to satisfy his sexual needs. His fault lay rather in his fatal domination by this woman, for his grandfather would never have tolerated it.

Comparatively little is known about Alice Perrers. She was clever, avaricious and amusing, rather than beautiful, but the hostile author of the St. Alban's Chronicle is probably prejudiced against her when he alleges that in her later career whilst sitting on the judicial bench, she took bribes from the judges. He relates that she was the daughter of an Essex tiler and a former domestic servant, when it is known that her father was Sir Richard Perrers, a Hertfordshire landowner. Sir Richard had indulged in a bitter dispute with the powerful St. Alban's Abbey concerning land, which would explain the two hostile references to his daughter. Edward lavished on the avaricious Alice valuable property in London and Egremont Castle. Alice went through a form of marriage with Sir William de Windsor, a castle official, but Edward later swore with an oath, when at loggerheads with the Commons, that he had no knowledge of it. To rid himself of de Windsor, Edward twice sent him a lieutenant to Ireland.

For some years the noble Queen Philippa had been ill of a dropsical malady and by August 1369, lay dying in Windsor Castle, where the King visited her. Froissart's moving account of her death is worth relating:

> And the good lady, whanne she knew and percyved that there was no remedy but dethe, she desyred to speke with the Kynge her husbande, and whanne he was before her, she put out of her bedde her right hand, and toke the Kynge by his right hand, who was right sorrowful at his hert, than she said, 'Sir, we have in peace eniowed great prosperity, used all our tyme toguyder. Sir, I pray you at our departyng that ye wyll grant thre deyres (desires).' The King ryght sorrowfully wepyng sayd, 'Madam, desyr what ye wyll, I graunt it.' She then asked her husband to pay all her debts and to fulfil all such ordnances and promises she had made to the church. 'Thirdly, Sir, I requyre you that it may please you to take none other sepulchre whatsoever it shall please God to call you out of this transytorie lyfe, but besyde me in Westminster.' The Kynge all wepynge said, 'Madame, I graunt all your desyr.'[1]

All her sons were absent on the Continent except Thomas of Woodstock, the youngest, then fourteen, present in the death chamber.

Possibly if Philippa had lived, Edward's decline would not have been so precipitate, but it was hastened after her death. Aware of the King's subjection to a mistress, the country learned to despise him. However, there were other reasons for the deterioration in Edward's character. In Charles V, he confronted a far more formidable adversary than the chivalrous knight-errant John the Good (Jean le Bon) or his father, Philip VI. A study of the sixteen year reign of Charles Sapiens,[2] as he was called by the chroniclers, shows how he outwitted both Edward and the Black Prince by his cunning and political flair.

How fortunate for France that Charles the Dauphin succeeded his father in 1364, a king of a dismembered and divided country. He was certainly not the popular idea of a medieval monarch, leading his armies in the field. Charles's personal experience of war was to fly from the battlefield of Poitiers late in the day. Indeed, neither his wretched health nor his tastes fitted him to the active life of a soldier. Where Charles excelled was in his astute choice of commanders, particularly of Bertrand du Guesclin, whom he created Constable of France. From the first, Charles avoided pitched battles, as he had done when Regent, favouring guerilla and 'scorched earth' tactics.

Charles possessed all the love of luxury and magnificence of his father and Valois ancestors, possessing a marked sense of his royal majesty and excessively conscious of the duties of office.[3] He reconstructed the Louvre and Vincennes, building a fine country house at Beauté-sur-Marne and a town house, the Hôtel Saint-Paul near the Bastille. The bent of his mind was decidedly legal, causing Edward III to refer to him scornfully as a lawyer. Like his two younger brothers, the Dukes of Berry and Burgundy (John the Good's youngest son, Philip le Hardi, had been created Duke of Burgundy after his father's death in 1364), Charles loved beautiful things, jewels, plate and fine tapestries. His taste for books induced him to found an important library, and he took the trouble to get the Latin historians and political works of Aristotle translated into French.

Despite the cruelty and brutality prevalent in the fourteenth and early fifteenth century, this period produced magnificent patrons of art. Such were Berry and Burgundy, too engrossed in the acquisition of works of art to be consumed by ideas of war. Captured at Poitiers when only seventeen, Berry was an ungainly youth, possessing a square common pugnosed face and thick body.[4] Later, in France, he took an avid delight in filling his seventeen châteaux with exquisite, illuminated books, clocks, tapestries and other works. To gratify his æsthetic tastes, Berry mercilessly taxed the people of Auvergne and Languedoc when he was their governor. Thus we can picture him, an insatiable collector, dressed in his sky-blue robe, commissioning the Limbourg brothers to make that exquisite masterpiece the *Très Riches Heures*.[5] Nothing would satisfy him but the best. Hearing of a rare and unusual species of greyhound in Scotland, in his later career, he sought a safe-conduct from Richard II, Edward III's grandson, to allow four courtiers to travel there to bring him back a pair. Berry lived to the ripe old age of 76, not surprisingly, dying insolvent, in 1416. He is buried in the Crypt of Bourges Cathedral.

Burgundy possessed overwhelming pride and ambition, being more intelligent than Berry. Anxious not to be outshone by his brother, he, too, was always splendidly dressed, wearing a hat with plumes of ostrich, pheasant and bird of India. Not only had he a passion for collecting, but he was devoted to hunting, restlessly moving from estate to estate, and liking to sleep out of doors. Such was Philip le Hardi (The Bold), who as a boy had been King Edward's prisoner in London and Windsor. He died in 1404. Today the visitor to Dijon can visit the former palace of the Dukes and States-General of Burgundy, now the Musée des Beaux-Arts. No tomb can be more beautiful than the resplendent Philip lying on black marble, guarded by two solicitous angels with golden wings. The work of Jean de Marville, a sculptor and Claus Sluter.

Charles V, although no soldier, masterminded all the military campaigns throughout his reign. He wanted capable, guerrilla leaders rather than great generals, so he promoted Bertrand du Guesclin, Oliver de Clisson and the Admiral Jean de Vienne among others. Froissart was truly astonished that Charles had heaped so much favour on du Guesclin, for on the eve of his accession he merely had the reputation of a captain of *routiers*, exercising no discipline over his men. This thin, ugly soldier with his uncouth appearance rose to high rank and gloried in it. He shared his King's interest in astrology, for Charles's court astrologer would advise him on the most propitious day to undertake campaigns.

Perroy had no high opinion of du Guesclin. He wrote of him:

In this mediocre captain, incapable of winning a battle or being successful in any siege of any scope, just good enough to put new life into the hands of pillaging *routiers* who recognised their master in him, swollen with self-importance and at the same time punctilious about chivalrous honour.

All the same, when Charles the Bad again rebelled in 1364, du Guesclin gained a brilliant victory over the Gascon contingents of the Caplal of Buch.

During 1361 England and France were again smitten by the Plague, but it was England the smaller country, that suffered most. Because of the difficulty in finding archers for its foreign garrisons, it was made compulsory for all able-bodied men to pursue archery practice on Saints' days and holidays. Two years later (1363), the Prince of Wales was sent to govern Aquitaine as a sovereign and independent prince. Of his court the Chandos herald wrote:

There abodes all nobleness, all joy and jollity, largess, gentleness and honour, and all his subjects and all his men loved him right dearly.[6]

The Prince, however, was much criticized, for the extravagance of his court, and it was unwise of him to raise taxes, particularly the detested *fouage* or hearth tax to maintain its splendour. With their growing sense of nationalism, this tax was deeply resented by the merchants and the Gallic peasants. Furthermore, the Prince sadly lacked sensitivity in appointing so many English lords to administer the province. It was natural for the Gascon nobles to be deeply offended that foreigners should hold the highest offices in their ancient duchy.

True, Sir John Chandos, never far from his master, was High Constable of Aquitaine and much loved for his good sense and chivalry, but the offices of High Seneschal of Aquitaine, the Seneschal of Poitou and other offices were held by men of less calibre.

Presiding over this magnificent court together with her husband was the enchanting Princess Joan. During these years in Gascony she was to give birth to two infant Princes, Edward of Angoulême and Richard of Bordeaux, born on Epiphany day 1367 (January 6th).

During 1366 civil war erupted in Spain when Don Enrico of Trasmara, bastard half-brother of Pedro the Cruel, succeeded temporarily in ousting the legitimate sovereign from the throne. Pedro fled to Corunna where he appealed to the Black Prince for aid. Seeing himself "as the knight-errant of Christendom, leading a righteous war"[7] as Sir Arthur Bryant wrote, the Black Prince prepared to cross the Pyrenees, supported by a thousand archers from the forests of Cheshire and the north. Seizing his opportunity to oppose the prince, Charles V sent troops under Bertrand du Guesclin to help the Bastard, seeing him as a future ally against the English. Probably the Prince of Wales was influenced by realism as well as chivalry. By coming to Pedro's aid he would deny France the Castilian navy.

The Battle of Nájera was the last of the Black Prince's great victories, fought on April 3rd 1367, but it was to end in disillusion and calamity.

Those who doubt his devotion to his wife Princess Joan, will think otherwise when they read his account of the battle (written April 5th):

> My dearest and truest sweetheart and beloved companion. So we put ourselves into battle order, and did so well by the will and grace of God that the Bastard and all his men were defeated...and between five and six thousand of those who fought were killed...and there were plenty of prisoners...among others are Don Sancho, the Bastard's brother, the Count of Denia and Bertrand de Guesclin.[8]

It was the Windsor Herald who brought King Edward in England good news of his first-born son on or before June 12th 1367, because on that day he was granted a reward for his services - an annuity of 20 marks. However, Edward had heard of the victory by the end of April when he ordered Simon Langham Archbishop of Canterbury to publicize the triumph.

The Black Prince temporarily restored Pedro to his throne, but he was unable to pay the Prince of Wales the 600,000 florins he had promised. Consequently the Principality was forced to shoulder the enormous cost of the campaign. His only reward were a few jewels, including a great ruby, now among the English Crown Jewels.

Undoubtedly the most disastrous repercussion of Nájera was the ruined health of the Black Prince and of many of his troops, victims of dysentery caused by the burning heat that followed the severe cold of a Castilian winter. Back in Bordeaux, enfeebled by disease, the Prince at the beginning of 1368 imposed a five year *fouage* or tax on every hearth in the principality to meet his war liabilities. He would have been wiser to listen to Chandos, who advised his master to discontinue the tax altogether. So, Chandos retired to his estates in Normandy.

Despite King Edward's shrewd advice to his son to drop the *fouage* the Prince refused to do so. Now matters came to a head when two of the most powerful lords of Guyenne, lords of Armagnac and Albret refused to allow the tax to be levied in their domains. Firstly they appealed to the King of England, then without waiting for his reply, to the King of France. Acting with his customary caution, on December 3rd 1368, Charles accepted their appeal, having already laid their case before the *parlement* of Paris. He announced with legal chicanery that since King Edward had failed to ratify the renunciation of his claim to the French throne, his father's surrender of the overlordship of Aquitaine had never become effective. Aquitaine was therefore still part of France. The English retorted by claiming that this was a clear violation of the Treaty of Brétigny.

In the middle of January (1369) Charles formally summoned the Prince of Wales to appear before the *Parlement*. Froissart relates the Prince's reply. After swearing a mighty oath he exclaimed:

> We shall readily go to Paris on the way when we are summoned, since it is so ordered by the King of France, but it will be helmet on head, with sixty thousand men in our company.but he was no longer able to take more

positive action. The King of France now felt himself strong enough to send a formal defiance to Edward, delivered by a 'sculleon', according to Froissart. When the discontented Gascons revolted against the English, more than nine hundred castles and towns repudiated their allegiance. In the north, Abbeville was overrun and the county of Ponthieu and other districts fell to the French.

One of the most serious reverses suffered by the English was the death, in 1370, in a skirmish near Poitiers, of Sir John Chandos, who was universally loved. Froissart praises him, saying he was "courteous and benign, amiable, liberal, preux (skilled), sage and true in all causes". He exercised a moderating influence over the Black Prince, not always successfully. One wonders if he had lived whether he might have used his influence to restrain him from ordering the terrible massacre at Limoges.

He was, however, by 1370 a very sick man, unable to mount his horse and having to be borne by litter. It is not possible to excuse the Prince's behaviour at Limoges, though his state of health probably explains it. It will always remain a blemish on his reputation for chivalry. He could not forgive its bishop, Jehan de Cros, once an intimate friend and godfather of his son Edward, from deserting his cause.

At the end of August, Limoges was surrendered to the Duke of Berry, after the townsmen had risen against the English garrison. Swearing by his father's soul that he would make the people pay dearly for this, the Black Prince rose from his sick-bed at Angoulême and was carried in his litter to the city with his army. For a month the English manned the walls. Froissart relates:

> Then the Prince, the Duke of Lancaster (John of Gaunt), the Earl of Cambridge (Edmund of Langley) and Sir Guichard d'Angle...burst into the city, followed by pillagers on foot, all in a mood to wreak havoc and do murder, killing indiscriminately for those were their orders...Men, women and children flung themselves to their knees before the Prince, crying 'Have mercy on us, gentle Sir!'

However, he was so inflamed with anger that he would not listen. More than three thousand citizens were killed. Only the three leaders of the garrison survived, Sir Jean de Villemur, Sir Hugues de la Roche and Roger de Beaumont, and only because they gallantly engaged in personal combat with John of Gaunt, his brother, Cambridge and the Earl of Pembroke (Edward III's son-in-law), and surrendered as prisoners. When the bishop was brought before the Black Prince, he grimly exclaimed: "By God and St. George I will have his head cut off."[9] But his life was saved by John of Gaunt.

Perhaps it would have been better if the Prince of Wales had died immediately after Nájera, for the massacre besmirches his memory, sullying his reputation. There only remained the bitter last years, the pain of illness, a tragedy for such an active man, once the hero of the nation. On the advice of his surgeon, the Prince of Wales returned to England in January 1371, together with Princess Joan and his infant son Richard, finally resigning his principality, in October of the following year. He lived mostly in his castle in Berkhamsted in Hertfordshire.

Once only did King Edward and his sick son make a final effort to go on campaign. In the late summer of 1372, Edward, on board *The Grace-Dieu*, and the Black Prince, sailed from Sandwich, but incessant storms and contrary winds forced the expedition to return to port. It had cost the enormous sum of £900,000.[10] "God and St. George help us" exclaimed Edward. "There was never so evil a King in France as there is now nor ever one who gave me such trouble!"[11] How he must have wished he was dealing with John the Good. It was to be the old king's last warlike expedition.

The early 1370s were the years of Charles V's successes. One factor helpful to the King of France was his alliance with Castile. He had succeeded in firmly setting Enrico of Trasmara, the Bastard, on the throne of Spain, England's enemy. Thirty years ago Edward had won the great naval victory at Sluys, but in his obsession for military glory he had somewhat neglected the navy. When a large English fleet attempted to relieve La Rochelle, whose governor was the Earl of Pembroke, now Lieutenant of Aquitaine, the combined fleets of France and

Castile vanquished the English fleet. Henceforward, much to England's embarrassment, the Bay of Biscay lay in French and Castilian hands, resulting in the loss of the Gascon wine trade.

John of Gaunt, the Black Prince's younger brother, was no great soldier, but he could be described as an all-powerful subject, possessing his luxurious palace in London, the Savoy, and enormous estates throughout England. After the early death of his first wife Blanche, he had married Katherine, the eldest daughter of Pedro the Cruel of Castile. His grand *chevauchée* in France in 1373, proved a costly failure. Leading an army of more than ten thousand men, the Duke of Lancaster advanced through Calais, Artois, Champagne and Morvan, finally arriving at Bordeaux with six thousand starving troops.

It accomplished very little, except possibly saving that city. Thousands of horses perished. At the beginning of 1374, all that remained of England's mighty conquests in France, was Calais and a small coastal strip between Bordeaux and Bayonne.

In his dotage and old age, Edward appears rather a pitiful character. We think of him with his long flowing white beard as he appears in his effigy in Westminster Abbey. Like his eldest son, he had lived too long on his fame. Better for Edward, perhaps, if he had died soon after Brétigny, unaware that most of his conquest of France would be lost in the ensuing years.

In many respects Edward's reign was glorious. One important result emanating from the long wars with France was the flowering of English literature. No longer was French the predominant language of government and literature. The most famous of these writers and poets working in their native language was Geoffrey Chaucer, though *The Canterbury Tales* was not written until the reign of Richard II, Edward's grandson.

One of the finest poets of the fourteenth century was Laurence Minot, probably a Yorkshireman, for the dialect of his poems is northern. He has been described as a jingoistic patriot in his outlook,[1] fiercely national in his sentiment, for he felt scorn, even hatred, for the foreigner. Thus as one might expect, he is mainly concerned with warlike events such as Edward III's decisive victory over the Spaniards off Winchelsea in 1350:

> How King Edward and his menze (company)
> Met with the Spaniards in the see.

Another poem is about the English capture of Guisne two years later.

Another important influence in establishing a national literature was John Trevisa, born at Crocadon in St. Mellion, Cornwall. He is best known as the translator from the Latin of historical works into English, for instance the works of the chronicler Ranulph Higden, a monk of Chester, who died in

1364. Trevisa, writing after Edward III's death, attributes the change to the death of many French teachers, owing to the Black Death. There were advantages as well as disadvantages, for pupils in the grammar-schools had barely any knowledge of French when travelling to strange lands. This new pride in English made it inevitable that by 1350, proceedings in the Sheriffs' courts would be conducted in English by command of the Mayor and aldermen of London.

The last six years of the old king's life were as inglorious as his earlier reign had once been glorious. The people, no longer sustained by victories overseas, became deeply disillusioned and critical of their rulers. Their malaise was largely of a spiritual nature, caused by the terrible visitations of the Black Death, making the people lose their faith in society. Yet Edward's long reign of fifty years had benefited most people in the community, including aristocrats, merchants, woolmasters, financiers and farmers. Homes became more comfortable, for as Sir Arthur Bryant wrote[2] hearths and chimneys took the place in rich men's houses of smoky open fires. Life became more elegant, for Flemish glass now appeared in traceried windows, and the new wealthy class of merchants could invest in fine manor-houses with private bedrooms, and their grounds containing spacious parks, gardens and fishponds. Many thought, however, including the poet Will Langland, that material prosperity merely bred spiritual decline and degeneracy. There was a great divide between rich and poor.

During Edward's reign a new wealthy class had arisen of masters and liverymen of merchant companies, Goldsmiths, Fishmongers and Vintners. These favoured people indulged in lavish hospitality, vying with one another to entertain lords and princes. Sir Henry Pickard, Master of the Vinters Company, one day in 1364 entertained King John of France and King David of Scotland, and the Kings of Denmark and Cyprus.[3] These important merchants such as Richard Lyons, were much hated by the people.

The most disliked nobleman of this period, however, was John of Gaunt, probably the most powerful man in the kingdom, owing to the dotage of the old king and the dominating influence of Alice Perrers. The Black Prince, too, was an invalid living at Berkamsted or Kennington. We think of the 'time-honoured' Duke of Lancaster as an elder statesman, but when he was thirty-five in 1375, it is evident he was widely mistrusted by the people.

There was even a rumour, almost certainly false, spread about by his enemies that he was a bastard, neither the son of Edward III or Queen Philippa.[4] The Queen on her death-bed is alleged to have confessed to William of Wykeham that John of Gaunt was really a porter's son of Ghent. She had given birth to a daughter at Ghent, but the infant princess had been killed in an accident. Fearing the King's wrath for the death of the infant, she had persuaded the porter's wife to substitute her son, born at the same time, for the dead princess. The story is obviously a fabrication.

Of all Edward's children, with the exception of the Black Prince, John of Gaunt seems most to resemble his father, with many Plantagenet traits of character.

He was hated not only for his failure in France, but for pressing very strongly the rights of the Crown against the rights of Parliament, a vital issue arousing passion during the last years of Edward's reign and that of his grandson Richard II. Many disapproved of the Duke of Lancaster's liaison with Katherine Swynford (widow of Gaunt's knight Sir Hugh), his children's governess, a woman nonetheless of high intelligence and tact. Though married to Constance of Castile, he was openly living with Katherine, who gave her lover three sons and a daughter. However, as events later clearly showed, John of Gaunt's ambitions lay in Castile rather than in England.

When Parliament reassembled during April 1376, they were in no mood to vote the various subsidies requested by King Edward. The so-called "good" Parliament was ready to defy the King. He met them in the Painted Chamber at Westminster, but they immediately withdrew. The Lords then reassembled in the White Chamber, while the Commons retired to the Chapter House of Westminster Abbey. The appointment of their speaker Sir Peter de la Mare , was sagacious, for he was bold and fearless, eager to champion their privileges.

They immediately demanded the dismissal of Edward's bad advisers, including William, fourth Baron Latimer, the King's Chamberlain of his household, a nobleman both intimate with Edward and John of Gaunt. Latimer held the important and lucrative offices of Constable of Dover Castle and Warden of the Cinque Ports. Three years earlier he had been appointed to negotiate with King Ferdinand of Portugal.

Parliament's impeachment of Latimer was the earliest to be recorded. He was accused of oppression in Brittany, of having sold the Castle of St. Sauveur to the enemy, of taking bribes for the release of captured ships and of obtaining money together with Richard Lyons, the important merchant mentioned earlier, from the Crown by the payment of fictitious loans. Latimer was ordered to be fined and imprisoned at the King's pleasure and at the request of the Commons removed from his office and from the royal Council. Lyons, who was detested by the people, was condemned to forfeiture and imprisonment. The surviving evidence is not sufficient to show whether they were guilty or not, but the Commons certainly believed they were.[5]

The attack on the king's mistress Alice Perrers, was tantamount to a personal attack on the king. It is very likely that as she completely dominated her royal lover and the Court, she tampered with the course of justice and she certainly abused her position by her avarice and love of gold. One of the victims of her oppression was the Abbey of St. Albans, to be regarded as highly prejudiced against this lady. She is known to have gone through a form of marriage with Sir William de Windsor, one of the castle officials, but Edward swore on oath, after the Commons petitioned against her in 1376, that he knew nothing of it. To get rid of Sir William, however, the king sent him to Ireland as lieutenant, where he was a failure. Alice Perrers was accused not only with interfering with the Courts of Justice, but of embezzling £3,000 a year from the Treasury and loading King Edward with dishonour. The king weakly acquiesced when the Commons petitioned that Alice should be banished the Court; he merely asked them not to deal harshly with her. However, they insisted that her property be confiscated. It is unlikely that John of Gaunt protested much at the temporary downfall of Alice Perrers, for after his father's death he obtained a grant (afterwards surrendered) of her forfeited property in London. She owned valuable property, including Egremont Castle, and elsewhere in London, and is known to have had financial dealings with William of Wykeham, accused of accepting bribes from her and various magnates.

In the middle of these troubles there died at the Palace of Westminster on July 8th, Edward the Black Prince, to be mourned not only in England, but throughout Europe. Even his enemy, Charles V of France "dyd his obsequy reverently in the holy chapell of the Paleys of Paris", according to Froissart. It is appropriate that he should be buried in Canterbury Cathedral, for he had a fondness for that city. His tomb is a superb example of Plantagenet craftsmanship and he is clad there in his armour, his dead eyes having a kind of subdued grandeur. Whether or not the Prince of Wales was opposed to the Court party and his father's government is uncertain, but since 1370 he had been unable to take an active part in affairs of state. Joshua Barnes, his father's first biographer, considered that the Prince of Wales "died too soon for the English nation, who had conceited much happiness to itself under his expected government and also for his Father, who desired above all things to leave so great a successor behind him..." There is no reason to believe, however, that the Black Prince would have dealt effectively with the terrible problems bequeathed to Edward III's grandson. An astrologer, named John Cadbury, had noted just before the Black Prince's death, evil aspects in the planets, a bad opposition of Saturn and Jupiter in Aquarius and Leo signifying calamity.

Froissart relates that after the Feast of St. Michael,

When the obsequy of the Prince was done and fynisshed, than the Kyng of Englande made to be known to his sones, the Dukes of Lancaster, the Earl of Cambridge (Edmund of Langley) and the Lord Thomas the youngest (the future Duke of Gloucester) and to all the Barons, Earls, prelates and knights of England, how that the younge Richard should be Kyng after his disease and caused them all solemnly to maintain him.

In fact the last act of the "Good" Parliament had been that the young Prince Richard, aged nine, should be introduced to Parliament immediately, for they feared mistakenly that John of Gaunt had designs on the throne.

Even his biographer wrote that John of Gaunt's "thirst for revenge hurried him into a course of action which violated law and justice alike".[6] Arrogant and reactionary as he was, the Duke of Lancaster had no sensitivity as to the sentiments of the 74 knights of the Shires and the 200 burgesses of the towns, who were members of the Commons. "What do these base and unnoble knightes attempt?" he complained to Lord Henry Percy. "Do they thynke they be kynges or princes of the land?"

Declaring the "Good" Parliament to be no Parliament at all, he declared its acts as null and void, dismissed the Council which the Commons had tried to place about the king, restored those who had been impeached, including Lord Latimer, and permitted Alice Perrers, the king's mistress to return to Court. Vowing vengeance against the man, who had with remarkable courage denounced Alice Perrers in Parliament, Gaunt had the Speaker, Sir Peter de la Mare, imprisoned in his own Castle of Nottingham. He now turned against his former friend William of Wykeham, so powerful an influence at Court, furious that the Bishop of Winchester had attacked with such bitterness Lord Latimer, advocating the peer's impeachment and accusing him of oppressing two of his retainers. For the time being, William of Wykeham was unjustly deprived of his temporalities and banished to within twenty miles of the Court.

When the last Parliament of Edward III's reign assembled at Westminster on January 27th 1377, it was packed with the Duke of Lancaster's partisans. The new Speaker was Sir Thomas Hungerford, a man whom John of Gaunt had much helped in his career, while Adam Houghton, Bishop of St. David's, an intimate friend, was the Chancellor. John of Gaunt's conception of Parliament was that it existed for the purpose of registering the decisions of the Crown and to vote supplies for the King's necessities. Consequently the Bishop of St. David's

145

panegyric consisted of a flattering reference to the nobility and graciousness of Edward's Queen when she had been dead for eight years. Most people were more concerned about Alice Perrers. Edward himself and his three sons that were still alive had their share of his praise. John of Gaunt, stung by the suspicions widely held that he had designs on the throne, made the Chancellor pronounce an eulogy on his father's heir, young Richard, also present, a boy of ten years. There was no difficulty in getting Parliament to vote for supplies for national defence against the threat of French and Scots invasion. A poll tax of fourpence was raised, but a few protesting members demanded the release of Sir Peter de la Mare.

John of Gaunt's support of John Wyclif, the great religious reformer, in his attacks on the worldliness and rapacity of the medieval church, was largely opportunist, but whatever his motives he gave much needed moral support to Wyclif's attempts to expose the deficiencies and evils of a corrupt church.

By the end of 1376 it was evident that Edward III had only a short time to live. Despite his extreme weakness, a few months before his death he held one last feast of the Garter at Windsor, where he created his heir and successor Richard, a Knight of the Garter. He bequeathed his grandson a terrible heritage, an England weakened by the rivalry of factions, deprived of nearly all her mighty conquests and at the mercy of her enemies.

To the last Alice Perrers was the most powerful influence around Edward, though the King's last will[7], dated October 9th 1376, had declared John of Gaunt his chief executor. Knowing this, William of Wykeham, anxious to recover the temporalities of his see, visited the King's favourite and offered her a bribe.[8] The Duke of Lancaster protested, but his confiscated temporalities were restored to the Bishop.

In one version of *Piers Plowman*, Will Langland retells the old fable in which the rats and mice decide to 'bell the cat'. Edward is the cat, while the knights and more influential men in the Commons were the rats and the lesser men were the mice. Worse was to follow, when the kitten (Richard II) came to the throne. One might speculate that the mouse was the Speaker, Peter de la Mare, but he was hardly a lesser man.

During the summer of 1377, after a reign of fifty years, Edward III had a severe stroke and died at his Palace of Sheen on June 21st. There are strong reasons for doubting the assertions of some historians that Edward was deserted as he lay dying by everybody except a solitary priest exhorting him to confess. The Monk of St. Albans is the main authority for maintaining that as the old man lay dying his mistress stole his finger-rings. Joshua Barnes, Edward's first biographer, could in no wise credit this. He wrote:

> But as for Dame Alice Perrers her rifling of his rings from his fingers, it is in no way credible. There was no such thing laid to her charge by her inveterate enemies. Wherewith this woman flatter'd the King that he should live until his speech fail'd him, whereby he neglected to pray for his soul as he ought to have done.[9]

It seems, too, incredible that Edward would have been left completely alone by his three surviving sons and his grandson. Richard was nearby at Kennington with his mother, and John of Gaunt and his brothers had easy access to their father. Some accounts relate that Edward talked fondly of hunting and falconry rather than spiritual matters.

His enemy Charles V gave this testimony on the King's death, that he had reigned most nobly and valiantly and well deserved to be added to the ancient worthies.

According to his promise to Philippa, Edward was interred near her in Westminster Abbey. His monument consists of a gilt bronze effigy lying on a Purbeck marble tomb decorated with miniature bronze effigies of his large family. An entry in the Calendar Patent Rolls[10] exempts from impressment a ship lying at Poole in Dorset with a cargo of marble intended for the tomb. The King's effigy is attributed to John Orchard.[11] He also had supplied six copper angels for Queen Philippa's tomb, made in her lifetime. The sculptor she employed was a fellow-countryman, Jean de Liège, a skilled craftsman, who had acquired a prestige for his work for Charles V of France.

Today we remember Edward for the glories of his reign rather than brood on his pitiful decline. For a fourteenth century monarch, highly successful for many years in his pursuit of conquest overseas, Edward was idolized by many people. However, there was a minority of outspoken people critical of the war even in his own age. They were both French and English. De Mézières, a Frenchman, courageously protested against the war, saying that the English were a scourge inflicted by God on the French for punishment of their sins. In 1375 a radical critic of the war, Thomas Brinton of Rochester, said that recent English reverses were a divine visitation for their past offences in ruining France. A Dominican priest, John Bromyard, in his sermons blamed warfare for causing corruption. Whatever benefits war produced, it caused greed and lack of scruple among the troops. Lastly the scholarly John Wyclif, the religious reformer from Oxford, whose growing influence among the people was to continue during the reign of Richard II, challenged any man's right to claim a kingdom and to hazard lives in pursuit of such a claim.

Less great than his grandfather, Edward was a pragmatic king possessing remarkable ability, but he was often the slave of his passions and this defect of character was finally to undermine his capacity to rule his kingdom.

Notes

Chapter I

1. *English Historical Review.* Vol. XII 1307-08, pp. 517, 518.
2. *English Historical Review.* Vol. 48 (1933). Professor Hilda Johnston, 'Eccentricities of Edward II.'
3. Act I, Scene 1.
4. The title was rightly reserved for a prince of the blood royal.
5. "She-wolf of France with unrelenting fangs that tears the bowels of thy mangled mate." Thomas Gray, *The Bard*, 1757.
6. According to *Edward II The Pliant King* by Hutchinson.
7. See p. 222.
8. *English Historical Review* Vol. 48 (1933)
9. Son of Edward I by his second marriage to Margaret of France.
10. *Some letters of the Kings of England now first collected from the originals in royal archives and from other authentic sources* edited by James Orchard Halliwell.
11. Act IV, Scene 2.
12. *The Chronycle of Sir John Froissart.* Translated by Lord Berners, p. 28.
13. Stow wrote that it consisted of 2,757 men.
14. Stow, *The Life and Raigne of K. Edward the Second*, p. 224.
15. Stow, *The Life and Raigne of K. Edward the Second*, p. 224.
16. Stow, p. 20.
17. P. 20.
18. P. 20.
19. Charles Lamb wrote that "the death scene of Marlowe's King moves pity and terror beyond any scene, ancient or modern, with which I am acquainted."
20. His translation of Higden's Latin *Polychronicon*.
21. See Introduction to Adam Murimuth's *Continuatio Chronicarum Robertus de Avesbury De Gestis Mirabilibus Regis Edwardi Tertii* edited by Edward Maunde Thompson.
22. *Ibid., Edward the Second, The Pliant King.*
23. *Chroniques I*, p. 247.

Chapter II

1. P. 42, *Chronicon Galfridi de Swynebroke* edited by Maunde Thompson.
2. Kent's confession will be found in French in the appendix to Murimuth, p. 253.
3. See Notes and illustrations p. 214, p. 35, Latin text.

4.   *Ibid.*, Baker, p. 35. *Fuit gravis conflictus inter cives Eboracenses et Hamonienses.*
5.   *The Chronicle of John Froissart* translated by Lord Berners, p. 60. *Le Bel's Chronicle* edited by J. Viard and E. Deprez, Paris 1904/05.
6.   *Ibid.*, Froissart, p. 57.
7.   Froissart, p. 49.
8.   Maxwell, *Robert the Bruce*, 1897, pp. 305-307.
9.   According to *The Chronicle of Lanercost*. It has remained in Westminster Abbey ever since, except for a brief period in 1950 when an attempt was made to remove it to Scotland. It was recovered after 90 days.
10. *Philippa and her Times* by Hardy.
11. *Philippa of Hainault* by Agnes Strickland, p. 46.
12. *Chronicon*, p. 44.
13. *The Life and Raigne of Edward III*, Stow's Chronicles, p. 219.
14. *Edward III*, Reverend W. Warburton, pp. 22 and 23.
15. *The Chronycle of Sir John Froissart*, translated by Lord Berners, p. 74.

Chapter III

1.   *The Hundred Years War* by Desmond Seward, p. 1.
2.   *Edward III and the Scots 1327-1335* by Dr Nicholson, (1965).
3.   See *Wyntown Orgynale Cronykel of Scotland* ed. David Lavis.
4.   *Edward III and the Scots* by Dr Nicholson, (1965).
5.   Brut, p. 283.
6.   *Edward III and the Scots*, p. 134. *English Historical Review. XIV (1931) p. 354.*
7.   P. 51, line 18. *Notes and illustrations*, p. 232; also Stow, *Life and Raigne of Edward III*.
8.   British Library MS. Harl. 4690 f.82.
9.   *Numerus estinctius Scotorum occiscrum excedetat sexagenta millia*, p. 52.
10. *Dictionary Of National Bibliography.* David Bruce.
11. Agnes Strickland. *Philippa of Hainault*, p. 555.
12. Desmond Seward. *The Hundred Years War*, pp. 30-31.

Chapter IV

1.   *The Age of Plantagenet and Valois* (1967) by Kenneth Fowler.
2.   *Edward III* by Rev. W. Warburton (1875) p. 59.
3.   Desmond Seward, *The Hundred Years War*, p. 32.
4.   *The Chronycle of Sir John Froissart.* Translation Lord Berners (1901) p. 102.
5.   *Ibid.*, p. 108.
6.   *The Chronycle of Sir John Froissart*, Berners, pp. 120 and 121.
7.   *A History of the Royal Navy* by Sir Nicholas Harris Nicolas, Vol. 1.

8.   *Ibid.*, Harris Nicolas, p. 47. Taken from Chronicler Avesbury.
9.   *The Chronycle*, p. 148.
10. *Ibid.*, p. 147.
11. Seward, *The Hundred Years War*, p. 46.
12. Sir Arthur Bryant, *Set in a Silver Sea*, p. 243.
13. *Ibid.*, *Letters of the Kings of England, now first collected from the originals*, edited by James Orchard Halliwell.

Chapter V

1.   *Journal of Medieval History XII* (1986). See Diana B. Tyson's article, *Jean Le Bel, Portrait of a Chronicler.*
2.   *Chronique Normande*, p. 49; also *Philippa of Hainault and her Time* by Hardy.
3.   *Tome I, Le Bel*, p. 271.
4.   Jean Le Bel says 6,000 archers.
5.   *Ibid.*, *Journal of Medieval History* (1986), Diana Tyson.
6.   See edition A and E Molinier de *L'Histoire de France* (1882).
7.   See *The English Historical Review* Vol. 87 edited by J.M. Wallace and J.M. Roberts.
8.   *The Chronycle of Sir John Froissart.*
9.   Tome II. Le Bel.
10. See Volume IX edited by A. Doubleday and Lord Howard de Walden, p. 84.

Chapter VI

1.   P. 73, Latin text. P. 246, Stow *Annales.*
2.   Froissart's date of the Foundation of the Garter in 1344 is almost certainly incorrect.
3.   See Margaret Galway's article in *The University of Birmingham Historical Journal I*, pp. 13-50, 1947/48.
4.   *The Court at Windsor* (1964) p. 17.
5.   For Hurley see Colvin's *The King's Works*, Vol. I, p. 130.
6.   *The King's Lieutenant*, Kenneth Fowler (1969).
7.   *Ibid.*, *The Crécy War*, Burne, p. 139.
8.   *Ibid.*, *The Hundred Years War*, Desmond Seward.

Chapter VII

1.   *The Hundred Years War*, Seward, p. 52.
2.   *Ibid.*, *The Crécy War*, Alfred Burne, p. 136.
3.   *The Chronycle of Sir John Froissart*, Berners, p. 278.

4.   Kitchen Journal, British Library Add. Mss. 25461.
5.   *Ibid., The Chronycle of Sir John Froissart*. Trans. Berners, p. 287.
6.   *Ibid., The Crécy War*, Burne, p. 172.
7.   Edward of Woodstock Prince of Wales was first called The Black Prince in *Grafton's Chronicle* (1569) in the days of Elizabeth I.
8.   *Ibid., The Chronycle of Sir John Froissart*, Berners, p. 295.
9.   *Ibid., The Crécy War*. Burne, p. 175.
10.   *Ibid., The Chronycle of Sir John Froissart*, Berners, p. 297.
11.   I recently visited the site of the Cross of Bohemia in Crécy, commemorating the bravery of John of Bohemia. The inscription reads: "Cette Croix, rappelle la fin héroique de Jean de Luxembourg."
12.   *Ibid., Baker Chronycle*, p. 261. Notes and illustrations; also Louardre *Histoire d'Abbeville I* (1848) p. 238.
13.   *Baker Chronycle*, p. 84.
14.   *The Chronycle of Sir John Froissart*, Berners, Chapter XXXIII.
15.   *The Crécy War*; also
      The Hundred Years War.
16.   Stow *Annales* 380.
      See also Notes and illustrations *Baker Chronycle*, p. 263.
      The Chronicler Robertus de Avesbury mentions the capture of the Small Castle of Liddel in Cumberland. All contemporary writers are horrified by the cruel slaughter of Sir Walter Selby in cold blood.
17.   *Ibid., The Chronycle of Sir John Froissart*, p. 313.
18.   *Life of Edward III*, p. 382.
19.   *Ibid., The Chronycle of Sir John Froissart*, p. 315.
20.   See Introduction XXXVII. *Political Poems and Songs*, edited by Thomas Wright, Vol. I.
21.   *Ibid., Political Poems and Songs*.
22.   *"Si modo plus dicam, faciam mihi tuna inunicam."*
23.   *"dum mel in ore gerent. Taurum retro pungere quaerent."*

Chapter VIII

1.   See Robert S. Gottfried's *The Black Death* (1983).
2.   Philip Ziegler. *The Black Death*, Penguin (1982) p. 47.
3.   John Harvey, *The Plantagenets*.
4.   P. 98 (Latin text), p. 270 Notes and illustrations.
5.   *Ibid.*, Ziegler, p. 125.
6.   Robert S. Gottfried, *The Black Death* (1983).
7.   Translated by Sir D'Arcy Power, K.B.C., from a transcript made by Eric Millar.
8.   Philip Ziegler's scholarly analysis in his *Black Death* is well worth studying.

Chapter IX

1. *Memorials of the Most Noble Order of the Garter* (1841) p. 1.
2. *Ibid., Memorials of the Most Noble Order of the Garter*. There have been eighty Ladies of the Order since the middle of the 14th Century when Edward III founded it. Queen Philippa and her eldest daughter Isabella were both Ladies of the Order.
3. P. 109, line 20. P. 280, Notes and illustrations.
4. *Ibid., The Crécy War*, p. 229.
5. *Ibid., History of the Royal Navy*, Vol. II.

Chapter X

1. *The Black Prince and His Age* by John Harvey, p. 15.
2. Most historians describe a *chevauchée* as a raid. The word really means a march or expedition of all arms.
3. *Ibid.*, Notes and illustrations Baker. Also p. 128, Latin text.
4. *Nouvelle Biographie Générale*, p. 483.
5. Alfred Burne in his *The Crécy War* estimates the English army amounting to 6,000 men, but it is possible they were 7,000.
6. *Ibid., The Chronycle of Sir John Froissart*, Berners, p. 366.
7. See translation of Le Baker, Notes and illustrations, edited E. Maunde Thompson, p. 301.
8. *Ibid., A Distant Mirror*, p. 149.
9. Notes and illustrations, Galfridi Le Baker, p. 303.
10. See p. 150 Baker, *"Mentiris inquit, pessime vecors, si me vivium posse vinci blasphemeris."*
11. *Ibid.*, Seward, *The Hundred Years War*, p. 90.
12. Notes and illustrations, Baker.
13. *Ibid., The Chronycle of Sir John Froissart*, Berners, p. 384.
14. *Ibid., The Hundred Years War*, Desmond Seward, p. 93.
15. *Ibid., The Black Prince and His Age*, Harvey, p. 100.

Chapter XI

1. *Histoire de Charles V* by R. Delacherral.
2. *A Distant Mirror* by Barbara W. Tuchman.
3. *Ibid.*, Seward, *The Hundred Years War*.
4. *Knighton Chronicon* II, R. Delacherral, p. 185.
5. *Ibid.*, Sir Arthur Bryant, *Set in a Silver Sea*, p. 285.
6. *Ibid.*, Froissart.
7. *Ibid.*, Delacherral, Tome 2, p. 192.
8. The Italians Villani and Bernardin Corio disagree as to the sums paid.

9. *Ibid., A Distant Mirror*, p. 191. However, it is more likely he acquired this title at Poitiers fighting with his father.

Chapter XII

1. See Mary Everett Green's *Lives of the Princesses of England*, Vol. 3, p. 164.
2. Wardrobe Acct. Edward III, Queen's Reign. *Ibid.*, Everett Green.
3. Widow of Aymer de Valence, Earl of Pembroke. She died in 1377, the same year as Joanna's father.
4. Her effigy, like Joanna's can be seen in Westminster Abbey on the south side of her father's tomb.
5. *Ibid.*, Green, Mary Everett, *Lives of the Princesses of England*, Vol. III, p. 298.
6. *Ibid.*, Barbara W. Tuchman, *A Distant Mirror*, p. 208.
7. Paul Johnson *The Life and Times of Edward III*.
   The English: A Social History 1066-1945, Christopher Hibbert.
8. *Life of Edward Prince of Wales*, London 1740, by Arthur Collins.
   Edward Prince of Wales and Aquitaine by Richard Barber (1978).
9. Shakespeare's Tragedy of *Richard II*, Act 2, Scene 2.
10. *The Count of Virtue* (1965) by E.R. Chamberlin.
11. *Ibid., The Count of Virtue* by E.R. Chamberlin, p. 43.

Chapter XIII

1. *History of the King's Works*, H.M. Colvin, Vol. I.
2. *Ibid., The Life and Times of Edward III*, Paul Johnson, pp. 160 and 161.
3. R.A. Brown in *History of the King's Works*, Vol. II (H.M. Colvin).
4. The moated Manor House at Platform Wharf, Rotherhithe. Eric Newton, Museum of London, Dept. of Greater London Archaeology. Reprinted from the *London Archaeologist*, Vol. V, No. 15 (1988).
5. *William of Wykeham* (1887) by Moberly.
6. *Ibid., William of Wykeham*, Moberly, p. 24.
7. *Ibid.*, Colvin's *History of the King's Works*, Vol 2, p. 796.
8. *English Castles*, R. Allen Brown, p. 135.
9. For a detailed study of St. Stephen's Chapel see Colvin, Vol. I, pp. 510-525, *History of the King's Works*.

Chapter XIV

1. See Berner's *Froissart*, Vol. I, p. 395.
2. Meaning Charles the erudite rather than the wise.
3. *La Guerre de Cent Ans* by Edouard Perroy, translated by W.B. Wells.
4. *Ibid., A Distant Mirror*.

5. They can be admired at Chantilly.
6. *The Chandos Herald. Life of the Black Prince.* Translated and edited by M.K. Pope and E.C. Lodge. London (1910).
7. *Set in a Silver Sea*, p. 294.
8. See A.E. Prince, *English Historical Review* 1926, pp. 415, 417. "A letter of Edward the Black Prince, describing the Battle of Nájera in 1367."
9. *Ibid.*, Seward, *The Hundred Years War*, p. 114.

Chapter XV

1. *The Triumph of English*, B. Cottle, p. 61 (1964).
2. *Ibid.*, *Set in a Silver Sea*, p. 306.
3. *Ibid.*, *Set in a Silver Sea*, p. 307.
4. Chr. Angl. 107. See also Agnes Strickland's *Lives of Queens of England. Philippa of Hainault.*
5. *Ibid.*, *John of Gaunt*, Armitage-Smith.
6. *Ibid.*, *John of Gaunt*, Armitage-Smith.
7. While he was at Havering-atte-Bower.
8. According to the Monk of St. Albans.
9. *History of Edward III*, p. 907.
10. 1387-1389, p. 127.
11. *Ibid.*, *History of the King's Works.*

Bibliography

Arderne, John, *Arte Phisiscali et de Cirurgia* (1412), translated by Sir D'Arcy Power, KBC.

Armitage Smith, *John of Gaunt* (1904).

Barber, Richard, *Edward Prince of Wales and Aquitaine* (1978).

Barnes, Joshua, History of Edward III *(1686)* Cambridge.

Beltz, George Frederick, *Memorials of the most noble Order of the Garter* (1841).

Brown, R. Allen, *English Castles* (1954).

Brut, Chronicle

Bryant, Sir Arthur, *Set in a Silver Sea* (1984). *The Island Peoples from Earliest Times to the Fifteenth Century*, Panther Granada Publishing.

Burne, Alfred, *The Crécy War* (1955).

Butt, Ronald, *A History of the Parliament. The Middle Ages* (1989).

Chamberlin, E.R. *The Count of Virtue* (1965).

Chandos Herald, *Life of the Black Prince* translated and edited by M.K. Pope and E.C. Lodge (1910).

Chronicon Galfridi de Swynebroke Le Baker, edited by Maunde Thompson (1889).

Cockayne's Complete Peerage, Vol. IX, p. 85 (1936).

Collins, Arthur, *Life of Edward Prince of Wales*, London (1740).

Colvin, H.M. *The King's Works* Vols. I, II, III, IV (1964).

Cottle, B., *The Truimph of English* (1964).

Delacherral, R. *Histoire de Charles V*.

Dictionary of National Biography, *David Bruce*.

English Historical Review, Vol. XII, pp. 517-518.

English Historical Review, Vol. 48, by Professor Hilda Johnston (1933).

English Historical Review, Eccentricities of Edward III, Vol. 48 (1933).

English Historical Review, Vol. 87 edited by J.M.Wall and H.N. Roberts. Antonia Gransden's article.

Everett Green, Mary *Lives of the Princesses of England* Vol III, (1849-1855).

Fowler, Kenneth, *The King's Lieutenant. A biography of Henry of Grosmont First Duke of Lancaster*, (1969).

Fowler, Kenneth, *The Age of Plantagenet and Valois*.

Froissart, John (Jean), edited by Berners, in many editions (1901).

Galway, Margaret, *Historical Journal of the University of Birmingham*.

Gottfried, Robert S., *The Black Death* (1983).

Grafton's Chronicle, (1569).

Halliwell, James Orchard, *Some Letters of the Kings of England now first collected from the originals in royal archives and from other authentic sources* (1846).

Hardy, *Philippa and Her Times*.

Harvey, John, *The Plantagenets*, Fontana (1967).

Harvey, John, *The Black Prince and His Age* (1976).

Hibbert, Christopher, *The English : A Social History 1066-1945, (1987)*.

Hutchinson, Harold, *Edward II, The Pliant King* (1971).

Jean Le Bel's Chronicle edited by J. Viard and E. Duprez, Paris 1904/05.

Johnson, Paul, *The Life and Times of Edward II* (1973).

Journal of Medieval History. Vol.XII, article by Diana Tyson, 'Portrait of a Chronicler'.

Kitchen Journal, British Library. Add. MSS. 25461.

Marlowe, Christopher, *The Tragedy of Edward II*, Act 1, Scene I; Act IV. Ed. H.B. Charlton and R.D. Waller (1933).

Maxwell, *Robert the Bruce* (1897).

Murimuth, Adam, *Continuatio Chronicarum Roberto de Avesbury (1890)*.

Nicholson, Dr. Ronald, *Edward III and the Scots 1327-1335* (1965).

Nicolas, Sir Nicholas Harris, *A History of the Royal Navy to the French Revolution* (1847).

Packe, Michael, *Biography of Edward III*, edited and completed by L.C.B. Seaman (1983).

Perroy, Edouard, *La Guerre de Cent Ans, translated by W.B. Wells, London, 1951*.

Plantagenet Encyclopaedia, General Editor, Elizabeth Hallam. Ancient and Medieval Book Club (1990).

Seward, Desmond, *The Hundred Years War* (1978).

The Annales or General Chronicle of England, first begun by Maister John Stow, London (1580).

Strickland, Agnes, *Lives of the Queens of England*, Philippa of Hainault, Vol.I, London (1851).

Stubbs, William (Dr.), ed. *Chronicles of the Reigns of Edward I and II*.

Tuchman, Barbara W. , *A Distant Mirror. The Calamitous 14th Century* (1979).

Wright, Thomas, ed., *The Political Songs of England during the reign of Edward III*, (1839).

Ziegler, Philip, *The Black Death*, (Reprinted Penguin Books 1988).

Index